# Modern Critical Views

Chinua Achebe
Henry Adams
Aeschylus
S. Y. Agnon
Edward Albee
Raphael Alberti
Louisa May Alcott
A. R. Ammons
Sherwood Anderson
Aristophanes
Matthew Arnold
Antonin Artaud
John Ashbery
Margaret Atwood
W. H. Auden
Jane Austen
Isaac Babel
Sir Francis Bacon
James Baldwin
Honoré de Balzac
John Barth
Donald Barthelme
Charles Baudelaire
Simone de Beauvoir
Samuel Beckett
Saul Bellow
Thomas Berger
John Berryman
The Bible
Elizabeth Bishop
William Blake
Giovanni Boccaccio
Heinrich Böll
Jorge Luis Borges
Elizabeth Bowen
Bertolt Brecht
The Brontës
Charles Brockden Brown
Sterling Brown
Robert Browning
Martin Buber
John Bunyan
Anthony Burgess
Kenneth Burke
Robert Burns
William Burroughs
George Gordon, Lord
  Byron
Pedro Calderón de la Barca
Italo Calvino
Albert Camus
Canadian Poetry: Modern
  and Contemporary
Canadian Poetry through
  E. J. Pratt
Thomas Carlyle
Alejo Carpentier
Lewis Carroll
Willa Cather
Louis-Ferdinand Céline
Miguel de Cervantes

Geoffrey Chaucer
John Cheever
Anton Chekhov
Kate Chopin
Chrétien de Troyes
Agatha Christie
Samuel Taylor Coleridge
Colette
William Congreve & the
  Restoration Dramatists
Joseph Conrad
Contemporary Poets
James Fenimore Cooper
Pierre Corneille
Julio Cortázar
Hart Crane
Stephen Crane
e. e. cummings
Dante
Robertson Davies
Daniel Defoe
Philip K. Dick
Charles Dickens
James Dickey
Emily Dickinson
Denis Diderot
Isak Dinesen
E. L. Doctorow
John Donne & the
  Seventeenth-Century
  Metaphysical Poets
John Dos Passos
Fyodor Dostoevsky
Frederick Douglass
Theodore Dreiser
John Dryden
W. E. B. Du Bois
Lawrence Durrell
George Eliot
T. S. Eliot
Elizabethan Dramatists
Ralph Ellison
Ralph Waldo Emerson
Euripides
William Faulkner
Henry Fielding
F. Scott Fitzgerald
Gustave Flaubert
E. M. Forster
John Fowles
Sigmund Freud
Robert Frost
Northrop Frye
Carlos Fuentes
William Gaddis
Federico García Lorca
Gabriel García Márquez
André Gide
W. S. Gilbert
Allen Ginsberg
J. W. von Goethe

Nikolai Gogol
William Golding
Oliver Goldsmith
Mary Gordon
Günther Grass
Robert Graves
Graham Greene
Thomas Hardy
Nathaniel Hawthorne
William Hazlitt
H. D.
Seamus Heaney
Lillian Hellman
Ernest Hemingway
Hermann Hesse
Geoffrey Hill
Friedrich Hölderlin
Homer
A. D. Hope
Gerard Manley Hopkins
Horace
A. E. Housman
William Dean Howells
Langston Hughes
Ted Hughes
Victor Hugo
Zora Neale Hurston
Aldous Huxley
Henrik Ibsen
Eugène Ionesco
Washington Irving
Henry James
Dr. Samuel Johnson and
  James Boswell
Ben Jonson
James Joyce
Carl Gustav Jung
Franz Kafka
Yasonari Kawabata
John Keats
Søren Kierkegaard
Rudyard Kipling
Melanie Klein
Heinrich von Kleist
Philip Larkin
D. H. Lawrence
John le Carré
Ursula K. Le Guin
Giacomo Leopardi
Doris Lessing
Sinclair Lewis
Jack London
Robert Lowell
Malcolm Lowry
Carson McCullers
Norman Mailer
Bernard Malamud
Stéphane Mallarmé
Sir Thomas Malory
André Malraux
Thomas Mann

# Modern Critical Views

Katherine Mansfield
Christopher Marlowe
Andrew Marvell
Herman Melville
George Meredith
James Merrill
John Stuart Mill
Arthur Miller
Henry Miller
John Milton
Yukio Mishima
Molière
Michel de Montaigne
Eugenio Montale
Marianne Moore
Alberto Moravia
Toni Morrison
Alice Munro
Iris Murdoch
Robert Musil
Vladimir Nabokov
V. S. Naipaul
R. K. Narayan
Pablo Neruda
John Henry Newman
Friedrich Nietzsche
Frank Norris
Joyce Carol Oates
Sean O'Casey
Flannery O'Connor
Christopher Okigbo
Charles Olson
Eugene O'Neill
José Ortega y Gasset
Joe Orton
George Orwell
Ovid
Wilfred Owen
Amos Oz
Cynthia Ozick
Grace Paley
Blaise Pascal
Walter Pater
Octavio Paz
Walker Percy
Petrarch
Pindar
Harold Pinter
Luigi Pirandello
Sylvia Plath
Plato

Plautus
Edgar Allan Poe
Poets of Sensibility & the
  Sublime
Poets of the Nineties
Alexander Pope
Katherine Anne Porter
Ezra Pound
Anthony Powell
Pre-Raphaelite Poets
Marcel Proust
Manuel Puig
Alexander Pushkin
Thomas Pynchon
Francisco de Quevedo
François Rabelais
Jean Racine
Ishmael Reed
Adrienne Rich
Samuel Richardson
Mordecai Richler
Rainer Maria Rilke
Arthur Rimbaud
Edwin Arlington Robinson
Theodore Roethke
Philip Roth
Jean-Jacques Rousseau
John Ruskin
J. D. Salinger
Jean-Paul Sartre
Gershom Scholem
Sir Walter Scott
William Shakespeare
  Histories & Poems
  Comedies & Romances
  Tragedies
George Bernard Shaw
Mary Wollstonecraft
  Shelley
Percy Bysshe Shelley
Sam Shepard
Richard Brinsley Sheridan
Sir Philip Sidney
Isaac Bashevis Singer
Tobias Smollett
Alexander Solzhenitsyn
Sophocles
Wole Soyinka
Edmund Spenser
Gertrude Stein
John Steinbeck

Stendhal
Laurence Sterne
Wallace Stevens
Robert Louis Stevenson
Tom Stoppard
August Strindberg
Jonathan Swift
John Millington Synge
Alfred, Lord Tennyson
William Makepeace Thackeray
Dylan Thomas
Henry David Thoreau
James Thurber and S. J.
  Perelman
J. R. R. Tolkien
Leo Tolstoy
Jean Toomer
Lionel Trilling
Anthony Trollope
Ivan Turgenev
Mark Twain
Miguel de Unamuno
John Updike
Paul Valéry
Cesar Vallejo
Lope de Vega
Gore Vidal
Virgil
Voltaire
Kurt Vonnegut
Derek Walcott
Alice Walker
Robert Penn Warren
Evelyn Waugh
H. G. Wells
Eudora Welty
Nathanael West
Edith Wharton
Patrick White
Walt Whitman
Oscar Wilde
Tennessee Williams
William Carlos Williams
Thomas Wolfe
Virginia Woolf
William Wordsworth
Jay Wright
Richard Wright
William Butler Yeats
A. B. Yehoshua
Emile Zola

*Modern Critical Views*

# GEOFFREY CHAUCER

*Edited with an introduction by*

## Harold Bloom

Sterling Professor of the Humanities
Yale University

CHELSEA HOUSE PUBLISHERS
New York

Cover illustration by Peterson Design.

10  9  8  7  6  5

Printed and bound in the United States of America

Library of Congress Cataloging in Publication Data

Chaucer, modern critical views.
    Bibliography: p.
    Includes index.
    Contents: The greatness of Chaucer/G.K. Chesterton
—The ending of Troilus; The effect of the miller's
tale/E. Talbot Donaldson—Can we trust the wife
of Bath?/David Parker—[etc.]
    1. Chaucer, Geoffrey, d. 1400—Criticism and
interpretation—Addresses, essays, lectures.
I. Bloom, Harold.
PR1924.C435  1985        821'.1        84-23082
ISBN 0-87754-606-1

# Contents

# Editor's Note

The essays in this volume are arranged chronologically in the order of their publication, beginning with G. K. Chesterton's remarkable and still unmatched estimate of Chaucer's originality and eminence. This is followed by the most crucial and essential of Chaucer's critics, E. Talbot Donaldson, represented here by two studies, one of *Troilus* and the other of the "Merchant's Tale."

The six remaining essays can be said to be in Donaldson's tradition of literary humanism in regard to Chaucer, as opposed to merely philological, historical or theological commentary. David Parker illuminates the powerful inner conflicts that make the Wife of Bath so complex and vital a human representation. Alice Miskimin brilliantly sets the context for Chaucer as the undoubted father of English poetry, while Donald Howard revitalizes our feeling for Chaucer's style and for the "idea" of *The Canterbury Tales*. The essays by Charles Owen, Saul Brody and Stewart Justman complement one another to give us a unified sense of the relations between literal and symbolic and between truth and fiction in the *Tales*, and since Chaucer is so comprehensive a writer, they also open up these difficult vistas of contrast throughout imaginative literature.

# Introduction

## I

Chaucer is one of those great writers who defeat almost all criticism, an attribute he shares with Shakespeare, Cervantes and Tolstoi. There are writers of similar magnitude—Dante, Milton, Wordsworth, Proust—who provoke inspired commentary (amidst much more that is humdrum) but Chaucer, like his few peers, has such mimetic force that the critic is disarmed, and so is left either with nothing or with everything still to do. Much criticism devoted to Chaucer is merely historical, or even theological, as though Chaucer ought to be read as a supreme version of medieval Christianity. But I myself am not a Chaucer scholar, and so I write this introduction and edit this volume only as a general critic of literature, and as a common reader of Chaucer.

Together with Shakespeare and a handful of the greater novelists in English, Chaucer carries the language further into unthinkable triumphs of the representation of reality than ought to be possible. The Pardoner and the Wife of Bath, like Hamlet and Falstaff, call into question nearly every mode of criticism that is now fashionable. What sense does it make to speak of the Pardoner or the Wife of Bath as being only a structure of tropes, or to say that any tale they tell has suspended its referential aspect almost entirely? The most Chaucerian and best of all Chaucer critics, E. Talbot Donaldson, remarks of the General Prologue to *The Canterbury Tales* that:

> The extraordinary quality of the portraits is their vitality, the illusion that each gives the reader that the character being described is not a fiction but a person, so that it seems as if the poet has not created but merely recorded.

As a critical remark, this is the indispensable starting-point for reading Chaucer, but contemporary modes of interpretation deny that such an illusion of vitality has any value. Last June, I walked through a park in Frankfurt, West Germany, with a good friend who is a leading French theorist of interpretation. I had been in Frankfurt to lecture on Freud; my friend had just arrived to give a talk on Joyce's *Ulysses*. As we walked, I remarked that Joyce's Leopold Bloom seemed to me the most sympathetic and affectionate person I had encountered in any fiction. My friend, annoyed and perplexed, replied that Poldy was *not* a person, and that my statement therefore was devoid of sense. Though not agreeing, I reflected silently that the difference between my friend and myself could not be reconciled by anything I could say. To him, *Ulysses* was not even persuasive rhetoric, but was a system of tropes. To me, it was above all else the personality of Poldy. My friend's deconstructionism, I again realized, was only another formalism, a very tough-minded and skeptical formalism. But all critical formalism reaches its limits rather quickly when fictions are strong enough. L. C. Knights famously insisted that Lady Macbeth's children were as meaningless an entity as the girlhood of Shakespeare's heroines, a view in which Knights followed E. E. Stoll who, whether he knew it or not, followed E. A. Poe. To Knights, Falstaff "is not a man, but a choric commentary." The paradox, though, is that this "choric commentary" is more vital than we are, which teaches us that Falstaff is neither trope nor commentary, but a representation of what a human being *might* be, if that person were even wittier than Oscar Wilde, and even more turbulently high-spirited than Zero Mostel. Falstaff, Poldy, the Wife of Bath: these are what Shelley called "forms more real than living man."

Immensely original authors (and they are not many) seem to have no precursors, and so seem to be children without parents. Shakespeare is the overwhelming instance, since he swallowed up his immediate precursor, Christopher Marlowe, whereas Chaucer charmingly claims fictive authorities, while being immensely indebted to actual French and Italian writers, and to Boccaccio in particular. Yet it may be that Chaucer is as much Shakespeare's great original as he was Spenser's. What is virtually without precedent in Shakespeare is that his characters *change themselves by pondering upon what they themselves say*. In Homer and the Bible and Dante, we do not find sea-changes in particular persons brought about by those persons' own language, that is, by the differences that individual diction and tone make as speech produces further speech. But the Pardoner and the Wife of Bath are well along the mimetic way that leads to Hamlet and Falstaff. What they say to others, and to themselves, partly reflects what they already are, but partly engenders also what they will be. And perhaps even more subtly and forcefully, Chaucer suggests ineluctable transformations going on in the Pardoner and the Wife of Bath through the effect of the language of the tales they choose to tell.

Something of this shared power in Chaucer and Shakespeare accounts for the failures of criticism to apprehend them, particularly when criticism is formalist, or too given over to the study of codes, conventions and what is now called "language" but might more aptly be called applied linguistics, or even psycholinguistics. A critic addicted to what is now called the "priority of language over meaning" will not be much given to searching for meaning in persons, real or imagined. But persons, at once real *and* imagined, are the fundamental basis of the experiential art of Chaucer and Shakespeare. Chaucer and Shakespeare know, beyond knowing, the labyrinthine ways in which the individual self is always a picnic of selves. "The poets were there before me," Freud remarked, and perhaps Nietzsche ought to have remarked the same.

## II

Talbot Donaldson rightly insists, against the patristic exegetes, that Chaucer was primarily a comic writer. This need never be qualified, if we also judge the Shakespeare of the two parts of *Henry the Fourth* to be an essentially comic writer, as well as Fielding, Dickens and Joyce. "Comic writer" here means something very comprehensive, with the kind of "comedy" involved being more in the mode say of Balzac than that of Dante, deeply as Chaucer was indebted to Dante notwithstanding. If the Pardoner is fundamentally a comic figure, why then, so is Vautrin. Balzac's hallucinatory "realism," a cosmos in which every janitor is a genius, as Baudelaire remarked, has its affinities with the charged vitalism of Chaucer's fictive world. The most illuminating exegete of the General Prologue to *The Canterbury Tales* remains William Blake, whose affinities with Chaucer were profound. This is the Blake classed by Yeats, in *A Vision,* with Rabelais and Aretino; Blake as an heroic vitalist whose motto was "Exuberance is Beauty," which is an apt Chaucerian slogan also. I will grant that the Pardoner's is a negative exuberance, and yet Blake's remarks show us that the Wife of Bath's exuberance has its negative aspects also.

Comic writing so large and so profound hardly seems to admit a rule for literary criticism. Confronted by the Wife of Bath or Falstaff or the suprahumane Poldy, how shall the critic conceive her or his enterprise? What is there left to be done? I grimace to think of the Wife of Bath and Falstaff deconstructed, or of having their life-augmenting contradictions subjected to a Marxist critique. The Wife of Bath and difference (or even "differance")? Falstaff and surplus value? Poldy and the dogma that there is nothing outside the text? Hamlet and Lacan's Mirror Phase? The heroic, the vitalizing pathos of a fully human vision, brought about through a supermimesis not of essential nature, but of human possibility, demands a criticism more commensurate with its scope and its color. It is a matter of aesthetic tact, certainly, but as Oscar Wilde taught us, that makes it truly a moral matter as well. What devitalizes the Wife of Bath, or Falstaff, or Poldy, tends at last to reduce us also.

## III

That a tradition of major poetry goes from Chaucer to Spenser and Milton and on through them to Blake and Wordsworth, Shelley and Keats, Browning and Tennyson and Whitman, Yeats and Stevens, D. H. Lawrence and

Hart Crane, is now widely accepted as a critical truth. The myth of a Metaphysical counter-tradition, from Donne and Marvell through Dryden, Pope and Byron on to Hopkins, Eliot and Pound, has been dispelled and seen as the Eliotic invention it truly was. Shakespeare is too large for any tradition, and so is Chaucer. One can wonder if even the greatest novelists in the language—Richardson, Austen, George Eliot, Dickens, Henry James and the Mark Twain of *Huckleberry Finn* (the one true rival to *Moby Dick* and *Leaves of Grass* as *the* American book or Bible), or Conrad, Lawrence and Faulkner in this century—can approach Shakespeare and Chaucer in the astonishing art of somehow creating fictions that are more human than we generally are. Criticism, perhaps permanently ruined by Aristotle's formalism, has had little hope of even accurately describing this art. Aristophanes, Plato and Longinus are apter models for a criticism more adequate to Chaucer and to Shakespeare. Attacking Euripides, Aristophanes, as it were, attacks Chaucer and Shakespeare in a true prolepsis, and Plato's war against Homer, his attack upon mimesis, prophesies an unwaged war upon Chaucer and Shakespeare. Homer and Euripides after all simply are not the mimetic scandal that is constituted by Chaucer and Shakespeare; the *inwardness* of the Pardoner and Hamlet is of a different order than that of Achilles and Medea. Freud himself does not catch up to Chaucer and Shakespeare; he gets as far as Montaigne and Rousseau, which indeed is a long journey into the interior. But the Pardoner *is* the interior and even Iago, even Goneril and Regan, Cornwall and Edmund, do not give us a fiercer sense of intolerable resonance on the way down and out. Donaldson subtly observes that "it is the Pardoner's particular tragedy that, except in church, every one can see through him at a glance." The profound phrase here is "except in church." What happens to, or better yet, *within* the Pardoner when he preaches in church? Is that not parallel to asking what happens within the dying Edmund when he murmurs, "Yet Edmund was beloved," and thus somehow is moved to make his belated, futile attempt to save Cordelia and Lear? Are there any critical codes or methods that could possibly help us to sort out the Pardoner's more-than-Dostoevskian intermixture of supernatural faith and preternatural chicanery? Will semiotics or even Lacanian psycholinguistics anatomize Edmund for us, let alone Regan?

Either we become experiential critics when we read Chaucer and Shakespeare, or in too clear a sense we never read them at all. "Experiential" here necessarily means humane observation both of others and of ourselves, which leads to testing such observations in every context that indisputably is relevant. Longinus is the ancestor of such experiential criticism, but its masters are Samuel Johnson, Hazlitt and Emerson, Ruskin, Pater and Wilde. A century gone mad on method has given us no critics to match these, nor are they likely to come again soon, though we still have Northrop Frye and Kenneth Burke, their last legitimate descendants.

## IV

Mad on method, we have turned to rhetoric, and so much so that the best of us, the late Paul de Man, all but urged us to identify literature with rhetoric, so that criticism perhaps would become again the rhetoric of rhetoric, rather than a Burkean rhetoric of motives, or a Fryean rhetoric of desires. Expounding the *Nun's Priest's Tale*, Talbot Donaldson points to "the enormous rhetorical elaboration of the telling" and is moved to a powerful insight into experiential criticism:

> ... rhetoric here is regarded as the inadequate defense that mankind erects against an inscrutable reality; rhetoric enables man at best to regard himself as a being of heroic proportions—like Achilles, or like Chauntecleer—and at worst to maintain the last sad vestiges of his dignity (as a rooster Chauntecleer is carried in the fox's mouth, but as a hero he rides on his back), rhetoric enables man to find significance both in his desires and in his fate, and to pretend to himself that the universe takes him seriously. And rhetoric has a habit, too, of collapsing in the presence of simple common sense.

Yet rhetoric, as Donaldson implies, if it is Chaucer's rhetoric in particular, can be a life-enhancing as well as a life-protecting defense. Here is the heroic pathos of the Wife of Bath, enlarging existence even as she sums up its costs in one of those famous Chaucerian passages that herald Shakespearean exuberances to come:

> But Lord Crist, whan that it remembreth me
> Upon my youthe and on my jolitee,
> It tikleth me aboute myn herte roote—
> Unto this day it dooth myn herte boote
> That I have had my world as in my time.
> But age, allas, that al wol envenime,
> Hath me biraft my beautee and my pith—
> Lat go, farewel, the devel go therwith!
> The flour is goon, ther is namore to telle:
> The bren as I best can now moste I selle;
> But yit to be right merye wol I fonde.

The defense against time, so celebrated as a defiance of time's revenges, is the Wife's fierce assertion also of the will to live at whatever expense. Rhetorically, the center of the passage is in the famously immense reverberation of her great cry of exultation and loss, "That I have had my world as in my time," where the double "my" is decisive, yet the "have had" falls away in a further intimation of mortality. Like Falstaff, the Wife is a grand trope of pathos, of life defending itself against every convention that would throw us into death-in-life. Donaldson wisely warns us though that, "pathos, however, must not be allowed to carry the day," and points to the coarse vigor of the Wife's final benediction to the tale she has told:

> And Jesu Crist us sende
> Housbondes meeke, yonge, and fresshe abedde—
> And grace t'overbide hem that we wedde.
> And eek I praye Jesu shorte hir lives
> That nought wol be governed by hir wives,
> And olde and angry nigardes of dispence—
> God sende hem soone a verray pestilence!

Blake feared the Wife of Bath because he saw in her what he called the Female Will incarnate. By the Female Will, Blake meant the will of the natural woman *or* the natural man, a prolepsis perhaps of Schopenhauer's rapacious Will to Live or Freud's "frontier concept" of the drive. Chaucer, I think, would not have quarreled with such an interpretation, but he would have scorned Blake's dread of the natural will or Schopenhauer's horror of its rapacity. Despite every attempt to assimilate him to a poetry of belief, Chaucer actually surpasses even Shakespeare as a celebrant of the natural heart, while like Shakespeare being beyond illusions concerning the merely natural. No great poet was less of a dualist than Chaucer was, and nothing makes poetry more difficult for critics, because all criticism is necessarily dualistic.

The consolation for critics and readers is that Chaucer and Shakespeare, Cervantes and Tolstoi, persuade us finally that everything remains to be done in the development of a criticism dynamic and comprehensive enough to represent such absolute writers without reduction or distortion. No codes or methods will advance the reading of Chaucer. The critic is thrown back upon herself or himself, and upon the necessity to become a vitalizing interpreter in the service of an art whose burden is only to carry more life forward into a time without boundaries.

# G. K. CHESTERTON

# The Greatness of Chaucer

It is beginning to be realized that the English are the eccentrics of the earth. They have produced an unusually large proportion of what they used to call Humorists and would now perhaps rather call Characters. And nothing is more curious about them than the contradiction of their consciousness and unconsciousness of their own merits. It is nonsense, I regret to say, to claim that they are incapable of boasting. Sometimes they boast most magnificently of their weaknesses and deficiencies. Sometimes they boast of the more striking and outstanding virtues they do not possess. Sometimes (I say it with groans and grovellings before the just wrath of heaven) they sink so low as to boast of not boasting. But it is perfectly true that they seem to be entirely unaware of the very existence of some of their most extraordinary claims to glory and distinction. One example among many is the fact that they have never realized the nature, let alone the scale, of the genius of Geoffrey Chaucer.

I say advisedly the scale; for what seems to me altogether missed is the *greatness* of Chaucer. Men say the obvious things about him; they call him the Father of English Poetry, but only in the sense in which the same title has been given to an obscure Anglo-Saxon like Cædmon. He also has been called the Father of English Poetry, though what he wrote is not in that sense poetry and not in any sense English. They say that Chaucer marks the moment when our language began to be formed out of French and Saxon elements; but they see nothing elemental about the man who did so much to form it. They say (probably falsely) that Chaucer borrowed from Boccaccio the notion of a framework of stories; and they admit that he brightened it a little by giving more personality to the tellers of the Canterbury Tales. They admit (sometimes with a faint air of surprise) that this fourteenth-century man was acquainted with the nature of a joke; they concede a certain courtesy and urbanity, and then generally turn with relief to digging up the old original dull stories which Chaucer made interesting. In short, there has been perceptible, in greater or less degree, an indescribable disposition to *patronize* Chaucer. Sometimes he is patted on the head like a child, because all our other poets are his children. Sometimes he is treated as the Oldest Inhabitant, partially demented and practically dead, because he was alive before anybody else in Europe to certain revolutions of the European mind. Sometimes he is treated as entirely dead; a bag of dry bones to be dissected by antiquarians, interested only in matters of detail. But in no common English ears, as yet, does his name actually sound as a thunderclap or a trumpet-peal, like the name of Dante or of Shakespeare. It may seem fanciful to say so, but the name of Chaucer has not yet completely achieved the sound of a *serious* thing. It is partly the popular sense that Early English is a sort of Pidgin English. It is partly the pedantic prejudice that medieval civilization was not civilized. It is partly a sheer incapacity to thank those who have given us everything, because we cannot imagine anything else.

The medieval word for a Poet was a Maker, which indeed is the original meaning of a Poet. It is one of the points, more numerous than some suppose, in which Greek and medieval simplicity nearly touch. There was never a man who was more of a Maker than Chaucer. He made a national language; he came very near to making a nation. At least without him it would probably never have been either so fine a language or so great a nation. Shakespeare and Milton were the greatest sons of their country; but Chaucer was the Father of his Country, rather in the style of George Washington. And apart from that, he made something that has altered all Europe more than the Newspaper: the Novel. He was a novelist when there were no novels. I mean by the novel the narrative that is not primarily an anecdote or an allegory, but is valued because of the almost accidental variety of actual human characters. The Prologue of *The Canterbury Tales* is the Prologue of Modern Fiction. It is the preface to *Don Quixote* and the preface to *Gil Blas*. The astonishing thing is not so much that an Englishman did this as that Englishmen hardly ever brag about it. Nobody waves a Union Jack and cries, 'England made jolly stories for the whole earth.' It is not too much to say that Chaucer made not only a new nation but a new world; and was none the less its real maker because it is an unreal world. And he did it in a language that was hardly usable until he used it; and to the glory of a nation that had hardly existed till he made it glorious.

I know not why the people who are so silent about this go about glorying in the fact of having painted Tasmania red in an atlas or introduced the golf of Tooting to the upper classes of Turkey. But it is certain that, while some of them have (if it were possible) overrated the greatness of Shake-speare, most of them have unaccountably underrated the greatness of Chaucer. Yet most of the things that are hinted in depreciation of Chaucer could be said as easily in depreciation of Shakespeare. If Chaucer borrowed from Boccaccio and other writers, Shakespeare borrowed from anybody or anything, and often from the same French or Italian sources as his forerunner. The answer indeed is obvious and tremendous; that if Shakespeare borrowed, he jolly well paid back. But so did Chaucer, as in that very central instance I have named; when he turned the decorative picture-frame of the Decameron into the moving portrait-gallery of the ride to Canterbury.

It is worth noting, touching that patronizing tone towards the childishness of Chaucer, that there is very much the same patronizing tone in many of the earlier compliments to Shakespeare. In the case of Shakespeare, as of Chaucer, his contemporaries and immediate successors seem to have been struck by something sweet or kindly about him, which they felt as too natural to be great in the grand style. He is chiefly praised, and occasionally rebuked, for freshness and spontaneity. Is it unfair to find a touch of that patronizing spirit even in the greatest among those who were less great?

Or sweetest Shakespeare, fancy's child,
Warble his native wood-notes wild.

I suspect Milton of meaning that his own organ-notes would be of a deeper and grander sort than wood-notes so innocently warbling. Yet somehow, as a summary of Shakespeare, the description does not strike one as comprehensive. Hung be the heavens with black . . . have lighted fools the way to dusty death . . . the multitudinous seas incarnadine . . . let the high gods, who keep this dreadful pother o'er our heads, find out their enemies now—these do not strike us exclusively as warblings. But neither, it may respectfully be submitted, are all the wood-notes of Chaucer to be regarded as warblings. There are things in Chaucer that are both austere and exalted, such as certain lines in his religious poems, especially his addresses to the Blessed Virgin; there are things in Chaucer that are both grim and violent, such as the description of the death-blow that broke the neck of the accuser of Constance. And if he only occasionally rises to the grand or descends to the grotesque, it is not obvious that he is the less like life for that.

These examples, I may say in passing, afford an opportunity to say a word of explanation, even at this stage, about the spelling and diction of Chaucer and how I have decided to deal with it. In this also Chaucer suffers from a somewhat unfair disadvantage as compared with Shakespeare. Much of Shakespeare, as a matter of fact, was actually printed in an old spelling which would make many familiar lines look fantastic or awkward. Shake-speare's old English was near enough to be easily modernized; Chaucer's old

English was just remote enough to make it hard to do so while preserving the accent and melody. Nobody can read it, indeed, without wishing that some of its antiquated words were in modern use. The wretched scribe, starving for descriptive terms, will find many which he will envy the scribe of the fourteenth century. Indeed, the two examples I have given themselves illustrate the point. There is no nobler image of the ideal, in the ideal sense of that vulgarized term, than that single glimpse in Chaucer:

> Virgin, that art so noble of apparail
> That leadest us unto the highë tower
> Of Paradise . . .

nor can I ever read it without a sort of vision, of a garden tilted on a remote turret and a woman in trailing raiment, splendiferous like a comet, going up a winding stair. But, incidentally, what a pity that we cannot say 'apparail', instead of being dismally reduced to saying 'apparel'. And, oddly enough, there is a similar detail in the other instance I took at random; for when the slanderer of Constance was 'strook' so as to break his neck-bone, we have the pleasing further fact that his eyes 'brast out of his head'; which is going about as far as grotesque violence will go. But will not the envious man of letters think pensively and tenderly about the possibilities of the word 'brast'? When the sensational novelist makes the hero burst the bonds knotted by the atrocious Chinaman, how much better if he brast them! When the comic novelist says that Mr. Pobbles burst his collar, how much more forcible if he brast his collar! For this reason there is every argument for leaving Chaucer's language as it stands, and even admitting its superiority for some of Chaucer's purposes. Nevertheless, for reasons which I shall explain more fully elsewhere, I propose in many cases boldly to modernize the Chaucerian language, and especially for the purpose that is immediate here: that of showing that Chaucer was great in the sense in which Matthew Arnold connected greatness with what he called 'high seriousness' and the grand style.

Let anyone knowing only the popular and patronizing impression of a merry gossip or warbling court minstrel suppose that he has presented to him without context of criticism merely such a verse as this, printed as I have printed it:

> Such end hath, lo, this Troilus for love:
> Such end hath all his greatë worthiness,
> Such end hath all his royal estate above,
> Such end his lust, such end his nobleness,
> Such end hath all the false world's brittleness:
> And thus began his loving of Creseid
> As I have told; and in this wise he died.

Nobody who knows what English is will say that that verse is not dignified. Nobody who knows what tragedy is will say it is unworthy of a tragic poet. The words and spelling are not exactly as Chaucer wrote them, but they represent with some reasonable worthiness what Chaucer meant us to read. Now if anybody is so excruciatingly fond of the expression 'swich fin' that he desires to mingle it with his daily talk, as I have desired to use 'brast' and 'apparail', it will be easy for him (by the laborious literary research involved in looking at the book) to discover that 'swich fin' is Chaucerian for 'such end' and to convict me of having poisoned the well of English undefiled. But I will modestly yet obstinately repeat that it does not give the modern reader an idea of the dignity, that was in Chaucer's mind and gesture, to repeat 'swich fin' five times; especially as we do not know how Chaucer pronounced it and are almost certainly pronouncing it wrong.

Here, however, I have introduced this quotation in a quotable form, in order to emphasize the fact that Chaucer was capable of greatness even in the sense of gravity. We all know that Matthew Arnold denied that the medieval poet possessed this 'high seriousness'; but Matthew Arnold's version of high seriousness was often only high and dry solemnity. That Chaucer was, in that passage about Troilus, speaking with complete conviction and a sense of the greatness of the subject (which seem to me the only essentials of the real grand style) nobody can doubt who reads the following verses, in which he turns with terrible and realistic scorn on the Pagan gods with whom he had so often played. I have mentioned these matters first to show that Chaucer was capable of high seriousness, even in the sense of those who feel that only what is serious can be high. But for my part I dispute the identification. I think there are other things that can be high as well as high seriousness. I think, for instance, that there can be such things as high spirits; and that these also can be spiritual.

Now even if we consider Chaucer only as a humorist, he was in this very exact sense a great humorist. And by this I do not only mean a very good humorist. I mean a humorist in the grand style; a humorist whose broad outlook embraced the world as a whole, and saw even great humanity against a background of greater things. This quality of grandeur in a joke is one which I can only explain by an example. The example also illustrates that clinging curse of all the criticism of Chaucer; the fact that while the poet is always large and humorous, the critics are often small and serious. They not only get hold of the wrong end of the stick, but of the diminishing end of the telescope; and take in a detail when they should be taking in a design. The Chaucerian irony is sometimes so large that it is too large to be seen. I know no more striking example than the business of his own contribution to the tales of the Canterbury Pilgrims. A thousand times have I heard men tell (as Chaucer himself would put it) that the poet wrote *The Rime of Sir Topas* as a parody of certain bad romantic verse of his own time. And the learned would be willing to fill their notes with examples of this bad poetry, with the addition of not a little bad prose. It is all very scholarly, and it is all perfectly true; but it entirely misses the point. The joke is not that Chaucer is joking at bad ballad-mongers; the joke is much larger than that. To see the scope of this gigantic jest we must take in the whole position of the poet and the whole conception of the poem.

The Poet is the Maker; he is the creator of a cosmos; and Chaucer is the creator of the whole world of his creatures. He made the pilgrimage; he made the pilgrims. He made all the tales that are told by the pilgrims. Out of him is all the golden pageantry and chivalry of the Knight's Tale; all the rank and rowdy farce of the Miller's; he told through the mouth of the Prioress the pathetic legend of the Child Martyr and through the mouth of the Squire the wild, almost Arabian romance of Cambuscan. And he told them all in sustained melodious verse, seldom so continuously prolonged in literature; in a style that sings from start to finish. Then in due course, as the poet is also a pilgrim among the other pilgrims, he is asked for his contribution. He is at first struck dumb with embarrassment; and then suddenly starts a gabble of the worst doggerel in the book. It is so bad that, after a page or two of it, the tolerant innkeeper breaks in with the desperate protest of one who can bear no more, in words that could be best translated as 'Gorlumme!' or 'This is a bit too thick!' The poet is shouted down by a righteous revolt of his hearers, and can only defend himself by saying sadly that this is the only poem he knows. Then, by way of a final climax or anticlimax of the same satire, he solemnly proceeds to tell a rather dull story *in prose*.

Now a joke of that scale goes a great deal beyond the particular point, or pointlessness, of *The Rime of Sir Topas*. Chaucer is mocking not merely bad poets but good poets; the best poet he knows; 'the best in this kind are but shadows'. Chaucer, having to represent himself as reciting bad verse, did very probably take the opportunity of parodying somebody else's bad verse. But the parody is not the point. The point is in the admirable irony of the whole conception of the dumb or doggerel rhymer who is nevertheless the author of all the other rhymes; nay, even the author of their authors. Among all the types and trades, the coarse miller, the hard-fisted reeve, the clerk, the cook, the shipman, the poet is the only man who knows no poetry. But the irony is wider and even deeper than that. There is in it some hint of those huge and abysmal ideas of which the poets are half-conscious when they write; the primal and elemental ideas connected with the very nature of creation and reality. It has in it something of the philosophy of a phenomenal world, and all that was meant by those sages, by no means pessimists, who have said that we are in a world of shadows. Chaucer has made a world of his own shadows, and, when he is on a certain plane, finds himself equally shadowy. It has in it all the mystery of the relation of the maker with things made. There falls on it from afar even some dark ray of the irony of God, who was mocked when He entered His own world, and killed when He came among His creatures.

That is laughter in the grand style, *pace* Matthew Arnold; and Arnold, with all his merits, did not laugh but only smiled—not to say smirked. It is the presence of such things, behind the seeming simplicity of the fourteenth-century poet, which constitutes what I mean here by the greatness of Chaucer. He was a man much less commonplace than he appeared; I think than he deliberately appeared. He had so great a faith in common sense that he seems to have accepted with a smile the suggestion of the commonplace. But he was not commonplace. He was not superficial. His judgments are sufficient to show that he was not superficial. There is perhaps no better example of it than his journey to Italy and probable friendship with Petrarch, who was crowned with universal acclamation in the Eternal City as the one and only supreme and universal poet of the age; nor indeed was the admiration of the age undeserved. Petrarch was a poet, a prophet, a patriot, almost everything except what he was called, the greatest genius alive. It is typical of the neglected side of Chaucer that he admired Dante more than Petrarch.

It may be questioned, in passing, whether this understanding is understood. Dante was very different from Chaucer; but he was not so utterly different as the sound of the two names would now generally imply. It must be remembered that people began to talk patronizingly of a cheerful or almost chirpy Chaucer, at the very time when they talked about a merely Byronic or melodramatic Dante. Those who see Dante as something to be illustrated by Doré might well be content that Chaucer should be illustrated by Stothard. But there was another Chaucer who was illustrated by Blake. There was an element in Chaucer that was symbolic to the eye of a serious mystic. A medieval writer actually said that Chaucer's *House of Fame* had put Dante into English. And though this is an extravagant exaggeration, it is not (as some would think) an extravagant contrast. There is much more of Dante in the description of Chaucer, as he is whirled aloft by the golden eagle of the gods, feeling that Thought can lift us to the last heaven with 'the feathers of philosophy', than there is in the ordinary nineteenth-century notion that Dante was a dark and lowering Dago who was really only at home in Hell. Chaucer caught sight of the eagle; his tale is not always 'of a cock'. Yet he is greatest perhaps with the cock and not the eagle. He is not a great Latin epic poet; he is a great English humorist and humanist; but he is great. The very case of the cock in the Nun's Priest's Tale is concerned with richer and deeper things than a mere fable about animals. It is not enough to talk, as some critics do, about Reynard the Fox or the Babrian origins. Just as they mainly insist that 'Sir Topas' is a parody, so they are chiefly struck by the fact that the fable is a fable. Curiously enough, in actual fact, it is either much more or much less than a fable. The interpretation is full of that curious rich native humour, which is at once riotous and secretive. It is extraordinarily English, especially in this, that it does not aim at being neat, as wit and logic are neat. It rather delights in being clumsy; as if clumsiness were part of the fun. Chaucer is not accepting a convention; he is enjoying a contradiction. Hundreds of years afterwards, a French poet was struck by the strutting arody of humanity in the poultry yard, and elaborated the same medieval jest, giving the cock the same medieval name. But the Chantecler of Rostand, with its many beautiful and rational epigrams in the French manner, has about it a sort of exact coincidence of mimicry, which fits it to the province of an actor. Rostand is pleased, as a stage manager, with the aptness of making a man act like a cock. Chaucer is pleased with the absurdity of making a cock act like a man. These are aesthetic and psychological impressions, about which nobody can prove anything; but I am pretty certain that Chaucer revelled, I might say wallowed, in the wild disproportion of making his little farmyard fowl talk like a philosopher and even a scholar. The chicken in question is hatched from the works of Aristotle and Virgil; the Song of Roland, or at least the Carolingian legend; and was also (it is reassuring to know) very properly instructed in the Gospels. In a speech of great eloquence, the fox is compared to Ganelon and Judas Iscariot and to the Greek who betrayed Troy to its downfall. The cock's oration involves a deep dissertation on the reliability of Dreams, and their relation to the problem of freewill, fate and the foreknowledge of heaven; all considered with a sensitive rofundity of which any chicken-run may well be proud. In other words, in one sense the very sense of all this is its nonsense; at least its aptitude is its ineptitude. It is always difficult to make the fable, or even the four-footed animal, go on all fours. In this case Chaucer does not care if his two-footed animal has a leg to stand on. It has to limp as well as strut; the whole fun of the fable is in its being lop-sided; and he only partially disguises his biped in feathers. Then, when the imposture is quite obvious, he delights in asserting it again, allowing, as it were, his cock to hide hurriedly behind the one feather it has left. I can imagine nothing more English, or more amusing, than this exasperating evasion. He launches a denunciation of Woman as the destroyer of Paradise, and then explains to the ladies, as with a bow and a beaming smile:

> If I the counsel of woman woldë blame
> Pass over, for I said it in my game . . .
> These be the cockë's wordës and not mine,
> I can none harm of no woman divine.

There is something intensely individual in this playing in and out of the curtain, and putting on and off of the feathered mask. It is all the more subtle because nobody who reads Chaucer as a whole will doubt that, despite his occasional and probably personal grumblings against some faithless or scornful woman, he did really have a respect for women, which was not merely a bow to ladies. But if there is something here of subtlety, there is also something here of scope or scale. There is a largeness and liberty in the humorist who gets such huge enjoyment out of the metaphysical chicken, and expands so large a world of fancy out of the little opportunity of the fable. That is the quality in Chaucer which I would here emphasize first, because it should be realized before we go on to the secondary matters of origins and parallels and interpretations of particular points. The mind of Chaucer was capacious; there was room for ideas to play about in it. He could see the connexion, and still more the disconnexion, of different parts of his own scheme, or of any scheme. In the first example of 'Sir Topas', he completes his own scheme with his own incompleteness. In the second example we find him taking the tiny opening of a trivial farmyard fable, to expand it into an almost cosmic comedy. He seems to see himself as a small featherless fowl talking about the riddle of Destiny and Deity. Both have the same quality, not very easy to describe, the quality by which a very great artist sometimes allows his art to become semi-transparent, and a light to shine through the shadow pantomime which makes it confess itself a shadowy thing. So Shakespeare, at the highest moment of two of his happiest comedies, utters those deep and not unhappy sayings, that the best in this kind are but shadows, and that we are such stuff as dreams are made of, and our little life is rounded with a sleep. I say that this deeper note does exist in Chaucer, for those who will start with sufficient sympathy to listen for it, and not be content with some crabbed inquisition into whether he stole something from Petrarch or wrote something to please John of Gaunt. For one thing is quite certain; nobody who takes Chaucer quite so literally, I might say quite so seriously, will ever understand him. There is a sort of penumbra of playfulness round everything he ever said or sang; a halo of humour. Much of his work is marked by what can only be called a quiet exaggeration, even a quiet extravagance. It is said, in the description of him, that there was something elvish about his face; and there was something elvish about his mind. He did not object to playing a kind of delicate practical joke on the reader, or on the plan of the book; and all this may be summed up here, for convenience, under the example I have given. He did not mind making his fable something more than fabulous. He enjoyed giving a touch or two to the story of a cock and hen; that made it look like the story of a cock and bull.

We shall see more of this double outlook when we come to the conjectures about his private life, and especially about his personal religion. For the moment the matter to be established is a matter of scale or size; the fact that we are not here dealing with a mind to be merely patronized for its simplicity, but with a mind that has already baffled many commentators with its complexity. In one sense he is taken too seriously and in the other sense not seriously enough. But in both senses, almost as many men have lost themselves in Chaucer's mind as have lost themselves in Shakespeare's. But in the latter case they are like children wondering what their father means; in the former, like beaming uncles, wondering what the child means.

I mean that in the popular attitude towards Chaucer, and to some extent even in the more cultured criticism of him, there is a curious and rather comic suggestion of 'drawing him out'. I have said elsewhere that to many modern Englishmen a fourteenth-century Englishman would be like a foreigner. These modern Englishmen do really treat Geoffrey Chaucer as a foreigner. Some of them treat him very much as Mr. Podsnap treated the foreign gentleman. It will be remembered that that worthy merchant not only talked to the alien as if he must necessarily be slightly deaf, but as if he was in every other way defective, and had to have things put very plainly to him in words of one syllable. Yet Mr. Podsnap was really encouraging the foreign gentleman; he was drawing him out. Only there was a general feeling of pleased surprise that there was anything there to be drawn out. Chaucer is treated as a child, just as the foreign gentleman was treated as a child; but I am sure that Chaucer was quite sufficiently subtle to be as much amused at it as the foreign gentleman. Hence it will be generally found, even now, that anything like a problem or puzzle in Chaucer is approached quite differently from a problem or puzzle in Shakespeare. When sombody finds one of the Sonnets as dark as the Dark Lady, he admits that it is just possible that Shakespeare's mind may have been slightly superior to his own. But he has made up his mind that Chaucer's mind must have been more simple than his own, merely because Chaucer lived at the most complicated and entangled transitional time in European history, and drew on the traditions of about four European literatures instead of one. We shall get no further till we allow for this central and civilized character in the medieval poet; for the fact that he knew his philosophy; that he thought about his theology; and for the still more surprising fact that he saw the joke of the jokes he made, and made a good many more jokes than his critics have ever seen.

There is indeed one character, which Chaucer shares with all the great ancient poets, which may in some quarters weaken his position as a great modern poet. There are many moderns who say that a man is not a thinker, when they mean he is not a freethinker. Or they say he is not a freethinker, when they mean that his thinking is not tied tight and fast to some special system of materialism. But the point I mean is much deeper than these mere quarrels about secularism and sectariansim. The greatest poets of the world have a certain serenity, because they have not bothered to invent a small philosophy, but have rather inherited a large philosophy. It is, nine times out of ten, a philosophy which very great men share with very ordinary men. It is therefore not a theory which attracts attention as a theory. In these days, when Mr. Bernard Shaw is becoming gradually, amid general applause, the Grand Old Man of English letters, it is perhaps ungracious to record that he did once say there was nobody, with the possible exception of Homer, whose intellect he despised so much as Shakespeare's. He has since said almost enough sensible things to outweigh even anything so silly as that. But I quote it because it exactly embodies the nineteenth-century notion of which I speak. Mr. Shaw had probably never read Homer; and there were passages in his Shakespearean criticism that might well raise a doubt about whether he ever read Shakespeare. But the point was that he could not, in all sincerity, see what the world saw in Homer and Shakespeare, because what the world saw was not what G. B. S. was then looking for. He was looking for that ghastly thing which Nonconformists call a Message, and continue to call a Message, even when they have become atheists and do not know who the Message is from. He is looking for a system; one of the very little systems that do very truly have their day. The system of Kant; the system of Hegel; the system of Schopenhauer and Nietzsche and Marx and all the rest. In each of these examples a man sprang up and pretended to have a thought that nobody had ever had. But the great poet only professes to express the thought that everybody has always had. The greatness of Homer does not consist in proving, by the death of Hector, that the Will to Live is a delusion and a snare; because it is not a delusion and a snare. It does not consist in proving, by the victory of Achilles, that the Will to Power must express itself in a Superman; for Achilles is not a Superman, but, on the contrary, a hero. The greatness of Homer consists in the fact that he could make men feel, what they were already quite ready to think, that life is a strange mystery in which a hero may err and another hero may fail. The poet makes men realize how great are the great emotions which they, in a smaller way, have already experienced. Every man who has tried to keep any good thing going, though it were a little club or paper or political protest, sounds the depths of his own soul when he hears that rolling line, which can only be rendered so feebly: 'For truly in my heart and soul I know that Troy will fall.' Every man who looks back on old days, for himself and others, and realizes the changes that vex something within us that is unchangeable, realizes better the immensity of his own meaning in the mere sound of the Greek words, which only mean, 'For, as we have heard, you too, old man, were at one time happy.' These words are in poetry, and therefore they have never been translated. But there are perhaps some people to whom even the words of Shakespeare need to be translated. Anyhow, what a man learns from *Romeo and Juliet* is not a new theory of Sex; it is the mystery of something much more than what sensualists call Sex, and what cads call Sex Appeal. What he learns from *Romeo and Juliet* is not to call first love 'calf-love'; not to call even fleeting love a flirtation; but to understand that these things, which a million vulgarians have vulgarized, are not vulgar. The great poet exists to show the small man how great he is. A man does not learn from Hamlet a new method of Psychoanalysis, or the proper treatment of lunatics. What he learns is not to despise the soul as small; even when rather feminine critics say that the will is weak. As if the will were ever strong enough for the tasks that confront it in this world! The great poet is alone strong enough to measure that broken strength we call the weakness of man.

It has only been for a short time, a recent and disturbed time of transition, that each writer has been expected to write a new theory of all things, or draw a new wild map of the world. The old writers were content to write of the old world, but to write of it with an imaginative freshness which made it in each case look like a new world. Before the time of Shakespeare, men had grown used to the Ptolemaic astronomy, and since the time of Shakespeare men have grown used to the Copernican astronomy. But poets have never grown used to stars; and it is their business to prevent anybody else ever growing used to them. And any man who reads for the first time the words, 'Night's candles are burnt out,' catches his breath and almost curses himself for having neglected to look rightly, or sufficiently frequently, at the grand and mysterious revolutions of night and day. Theories soon grow stale; but things continue to be fresh. And, according to the ancient conception of his function, the poet was concerned with things; with the tears of things, as in the great lament of Virgil; with the delight in the number of things, as in the light-hearted rhyme of Stevenson; with thanks for things, as in the Franciscan Canticle of the Sun or the *Benedicite Omnia Opera*. That behind these things there are certain great truths is true; and those so unhappy as not to believe in these truths may of course call them theories. But the old poets did not consider that they had to compete and bid against each other in the production of counter-theories. The coming of the Christian cosmic conception made a vast difference; the Christian poet had a more vivid hope than the Pagan poet. Even when he was sometimes more stern, he was always less sad. But, allowing for that more than human change, the poets taught in a continuous tradition, and were not in the least ashamed of being traditional. Each taught in an individual way; 'with a perpetual slight novelty,' as Aristotle said; but they were not a series of separate lunatics looking at separate worlds. One poet did not provide a pair of spectacles by which it appeared that the grass was blue; or another poet lecture on optics to teach people to say that the grass was orange; they both had the far harder and more heroic task of teaching people to feel that the grass is green. And because they continue their heroic task, the world, after every epoch of doubt and despair, always grows green again.

Now Chaucer is a particularly easy mark for the morbid intellectual or the mere innovator. He is very easily pelted by the pedants, who demand that every eternal poet should be an ephemeral philosopher. For there is no nonsense about Chaucer; there is no deception, as the conjurers say. There is no pretence of being a prophet instead of a poet. There is no shadow of shame in being a traditionalist or, as some would say, a plagiarist. One of the most attractive elements in the curiously attractive personality of Chaucer is exactly that; that he is not only negatively without pretentiousness, but he is positively full of warm acknowledgement and admiration of his models. He is as awakening as a cool wind on a hot day, because he breathes forth something that has fallen into great neglect in our time, something that very seldom stirs the stuffy atmosphere of self-satisfaction or self-worship. And that is gratitude, or the theory of thanks. He was a great poet of gratitude; he was grateful to God; but he was also grateful to Gower. He was grateful to the everlasting Romance of the Rose; he was still more grateful to Ovid and grateful to Virgil and grateful to Petrarch and Boccaccio. He is always eager to show us over his little library and to tell us where all his tales come from. He is prouder of having read the books than of having written the poems. This easy and natural traditionalism had become a little more constrained and doubtful even by the time of the Renaissance. There is no question of Shakespeare concealing or disguising his borrowed plots; but we do feel that he dealt with them as mere dead material, of no interest until he made it interesting. He did in a sense destroy the originals by making the infinitely more mighty and magnificent parodies. Even great originals sink under him; he comes to bury Plutarch not to praise him. But Chaucer would want to praise him; he always confesses a literary pleasure which may well conceal his literary power. He seems the less original, because he is concerned to praise and not merely to parody. There is nothing he likes better than telling the reader to read books that are not his own books; as when the Nun's Priest expansively refers the company to the numerous works dealing with the subject of Woman, which excuse him from justifying the sentiments of a cock or further analysing the defects of a hen. Perhaps, by the way, there is a Chaucerian joke, of the sort that is called sly, in making the Confessor of the Nuns (of all men) say that he, for his part, knows no harm about any woman. It is the same in any number of passages, as in that admirably cheerful passage that begins:

> A thousand timës have I heard men tell
> That there is joy in heaven and pain in hell,
> And I accord right well that it is so,
> And yet indeed full well myself I know
> That there is not a man in this countrie
> That either has in heaven or hell y'be,

and which goes on to explain that these things rest on Authority; and that we must depend on Authority for many things, especially the things of which we can only read in books. It is typical of the obtusity of some partisans that this passage has been quoted as evidence of scepticism, when it is in perfectly plain words a justification of faith. But the point is that Chaucer talks in that cheerful voice, or writes in that almost jaunty style, because he is not in the least ashamed of depending on 'oldë bookës', but exceedingly proud of it, and, above all, exceedingly pleased to testify to his own pleasure. This is a temper which will always seem 'unoriginal' to the sensational sectarian; or the quack with a new nostrum; or the monomaniac with one idea. Yet, as a fact of literary history, Chaucer was one of the most original men who ever lived. There had never been anything like the lively realism of the ride to Canterbury done or dreamed of in our literature before. He is not only the father of all our poets, but the grandfather of all our hundred million novelists. It is rather a responsibility for him. But anyhow, nothing can be more original than an origin.

When we have this actual originality, and then added to it this graceful tone of gratitude and even humility, we have the presence of something which I will venture to call great. There is in the medieval poet something that can only be conveyed by the medieval word Largesse; that he is too hearty and expansive to conceal the connexion between himself and his masters or models. He would not stoop to ignore a book in order to borrow from it; and it does not occur to him to be always trying to secure the copyright of a copy. This is the sort of cool and contented character that looks much less original than it is. A man must have a balance of rather extraordinary talents, and even rather extraordinary virtues, in order to seem so ordinary. As they say of St. Peter's at Rome, it is so well proportioned that it looks almost small. To the eyes of sensational innovators, with their skyscraper religions toppling and tumbling, and conspicuous by their crazy disproportion, it does look very small. But it is in fact very large; and there is nothing larger in its way than the spirit of Chaucer, with its confession of pleasure and its unconsciousness of power.

May I be pardoned if I insert a sort of personal parenthesis here? All this does not mean, what I should be the last man in the world to mean, that revolutionists should be ashamed of being revolutionists or (still more disgusting thought) that artists should be content with being artists. I have been mixed up more or less all my life in such mild revolutions as my country could provide; and have been rather more extreme, for instance, in my criticism of Capitalism than many who are accused of Communism. That, I think, is being a good citizen; but it is not being a great poet; and I should never set up to be a great poet on any ground, but least of all on that ground. A great poet, as such, deals with eternal things; and it would indeed be a filthy notion to suppose that the present industrial and economic system is an eternal thing. Nor, on the other hand, should the idea of the poet dealing with things more permanent than politics be confounded with the dirty talk of the 'nineties, about the poet being indifferent to morals. Morals are eternal things, though the particular political immorality of the moment is not eternal. Here again I can modestly claim to have cleared myself long ago of the horrid charge of being a True Artist. I have been mixed up in politics, but never in aesthetics; and I was an enthusiast for the Wearing of the Green, but never for the Wearing of the Green Carnation. In those days I even had something like a prejudice against pure Beauty; there seemed to be very much the wrong sort of betrothal between Beauty and the Beast. But, for all that, it is true that the true poet is ultimately dedicated to Beauty, in a world where it is cleansed of beastliness, and it is not either a new scheme or theory on the one hand, nor a narrow taste or technique on the other. It is concerned with ideas; but with ideas that are never new in the sense of neat, as they are never old in the sense of exhausted. They lie a little too deep to find perfect expression in any age; and great poets can give great hints of them in any. I would say no more of Chaucer than that the hints that he gave were great.

There is at the back of all our lives an abyss of light, more blinding and unfathomable than any abyss of darkness; and it is the abyss of actuality, of existence, of the fact that things truly are, and that we ourselves are incredibly and sometimes almost incredulously real. It is the fundamental fact of being, as against not being; it is unthinkable, yet we cannot unthink it, though we may sometimes be unthinking about it; unthinking and especially unthanking. For he who has realized this reality knows that it does outweigh, literally to infinity, all lesser regrets or arguments for negation, and that under all our grumblings there is a subconscious substance of gratitude. That light of the positive is the business of the poets, because they see all things in the light of it more than do other men. Chaucer was a child of light and not merely of twilight, the mere red twilight of one passing dawn of revolution, or the grey twilight of one dying day of social decline. He was the immediate heir of something like what Catholics call the Primitive Revelation; that glimpse that was given of the world when God saw that it was good; and so long as the artist gives us glimpses of that, it matters nothing that they are fragmentary or even trivial; whether it be in the mere fact that a medieval Court poet could appreciate a daisy, or that he could write, in a sort of flash of blinding moonshine, of the lover who 'slept no more than does the nightingale'. These things belong to the same world of wonder as the primary wonder at the very existence of the world; higher than any common pros and cons, or likes and dislikes, however legitimate. Creation was the greatest of all Revolutions. It was for that, as the ancient poet said, that the morning stars sang together; and the most modern poets, like the medieval poets, may descend very far from that height of realization and stray and stumble and seem distraught; but we shall know them for the Sons of God, when they are still shouting for joy. This is something much more mystical and absolute than any modern thing that is called optimism; for it is only rarely that we realize, like a vision of the heavens filled with a chorus of giants, the primeval duty of Praise.

# E. TALBOT DONALDSON

# The Ending of "Troilus"

One of Chaucer's familiar pretences is that he is a versifier utterly devoted to simplicity of meaning—for the reason that he considers himself, apparently, utterly incapable of complexity. He defines his poetic mission as the reporting of facts in tolerable verse, and he implies that that's hard enough to do. True poetry may, for all of him, do something much better but it is not clear to Chaucer exactly what it is or how it does it. He and *ars poetica* are, to be sure, on parallel roads, moving in the same direction; but the roads are a long way apart and are destined to meet, perhaps, not even in infinity. On the one hand, Chaucer, reciting his simple stories 'in swich Englissh as he can'; on the other, poetry, penetrating regions of complex significance far beyond the grasp of a simple straightforward versifier.

Chaucer's pretended inferiority complex on the subject of poetry must have stemmed from something real in his own life probably connected with his being a bourgeois writing for high-born members of the royal court. What interests me now however, is not the origin of the pose, but its literary value. For I think that Chaucer discovered in the medieval modesty convention a way of poetic life: that, by constantly assuring us, both through direct statement and through implication, of his inability to write anything but the simplest kind of verse, Chaucer creates just that poetry of complex significance that he disclaims striving for. In this paper I shall focus attention on the last stanzas of *Troilus*, where it seems to me that a kind of dramatization of his poetic ineptitude achieves for him a poetric success that not many poets in any language have attained. But I shall first consider briefly some characteristic Chaucerian 'ineptitudes' in his other works.

Modesty is endemic both with Chaucer in his own first person—whoever that is—and with his dramatic creations: none of them can do much

From *Speaking of Chaucer*. Copyright © 1970, 1977 by E. Talbot Donaldson. W. W. Norton & Co., 1970.

in the way of poetry. Like the Squire, they cannot climb over so high a stile, or, like his father, they set out to plough, God wot, a large field with weak oxen; or, if they are not ploughing a field, they're gleaning it, like the author of the Prologue to the *Legend of Good Women,* and are full glad of any kernel that their talented predecessors have missed. Or else, like the Prioress, they are so afflicted by infantilism that they speak no better than a child of twelvemonth old, or less. Like the Merchant and the Franklin, they are rude men, 'burel' men, they cannot gloss, they have no rhetoric, they call a spade a spade; they come after even such second-rate poets as that fellow Chaucer, bearing only *hawe bake*—pig food—and are reduced to prose, like the Man of Law in his Prologue. They can't even get the data down in the right order, like the Monk or like the narrator of the Prologue to the *Canterbury Tales.* Or, worst of all, as in the case of the pilgrim who recites the romance of Sir Thopas, their inability to frame a story of their own makes them resort to 'a rim I lerned a longe agoon', and when that is shot down in mid-flight, they have to take refuge in one of the most anaesthetic sermons that ever mortified a reader. If it is dramatically appropriate that they be capable rhetoricians, like the Clerk, they comply at once with a decree that declares high style to be inappropriate to their audience. In short, they seldom admit to more than a nodding acquaintance with the Muse.

   The normal function of the modesty convention is, I suppose, to prepare a pleasant surprise for the reader when the poem turns out better than he has been led to expect, or, at worst, to save him disappointment when the implied warning is fulfilled. This latter alternative is perhaps valid in some of Chaucer's tales, notably the Monk's. But the really important function of the modesty convention in Chaucer is to prepare a soil in which complexity of meaning may grow most fruitfully. That is, the narrator's assertion, implicit or explicit, of his devotion to the principle of simplicity, his denial of regard for possible complexity, results, by a curious paradox, *in* complexity; for the harder he tries to simplify issues, the less amenable to simplification they become, and, in artistic terms, the more complex and suggestive the poem becomes. To epitomize, the typical Chaucerian narrator begins by assuring you, either by a modesty prologue or by the notable simplicity of his man-ner—sometimes by both—that in what you are about to hear there will be nothing but the most straightforward presentation of reality: the narrator's feet are firmly on the ground, but he is no poet, and his control of anything but fact is weak. Subsequently the poet Chaucer, working from behind the narrator, causes to arise from this hard ground a complex of possible mean-ings, endlessly dynamic and interactive, amplifying, qualifying, even denying the simple statement: these draw much of their vitality from the fact they they exist—or seem to exist—either unknown to or in spite of the narrator; indeed, the latter sometimes betrays an uneasy awareness that the poem has got out of hand and is saying something he doesn't approve of or at least didn't intend, and his resistance to this meaning may well become an important part of it. That is, the ultimate significance of the poem derives much from the tension between the narrator's simple statement and the complex of implications that have arisen to qualify it.

The Chaucer who tells of the pilgrimage to Canterbury provides an obvious example of this tension between the simple and the complex. At the very beginning of the Prologue he lets us know exactly what we may expect of his narrative—namely what he saw with his own two eyes, and not an adverb more. And, as I have tried to show elsewhere, his prospectus itself is a miracle of stylistic simplicity, its pedestrian matter-of-factness supporting by example the limited poetic ideal that it is expressing. Yet it is because he has succeeded in persuading the reader to expect no more than meets the eye that, when he comes to the portrait of the Prioress, the poet is able to reveal to us the profoundest depths of that rather shallow lady. The narrator, to be sure, describes her flatly as he saw her, and what he saw was attractive, and it attracted the warm fervour of his love; but what he did not see was that everything he did see amounted to a well-indexed catalogue of the Prioress's shortcomings, which seen coldly would produce a kind of travesty of a Prioress. But because of his love for the woman, he is unaware of the satirical potential of his portrait, so that this potential, while always imminent, is never actually realized. One feels that if any one had pointed it out to the narrator, he would have been horrified, as, indeed, the Prioress would have been horrified if any one had pointed it out to her—and as even today certain readers are horrified when one points it out to them. And quite rightly, too, because of the great love that permeates the simple description. But the effect achieved by means of a narrator who resists complexity is of a highly complex strife between love and satire, between wholehearted approval and heartless criticism. These are factors which in logic would cancel one another, as a negative cancels a positive; but in poetry they exist forever side by side—as they also do in reality wherever there are ladies at once so attractive and so fallible as the Prioress. Indeed, the two factors, love and satire, unite with one another to form a third meaning—one which both qualifies and enhances the Prioress's own motto, *amor vincit omnia,* by suggesting something of the complex way in which love does conquer all. This occurs because the narrator, incapable of complexity, adheres rigorously to the presentation of simple fact.

The ways in which Chaucerian narrators enhance the meaning of their stories by missing the point of them are various. Occasionally, indeed, a narrator will rise up in the pulpit sententiously to point *out* or at least to point *to* what he takes to be his real meaning. The only trouble is that his aim is likely to be poor: he will suggest a meaning which, while it bears some logical relation to the ultimate significance, is at best no more than gross over-simplification. For instance, the Nun's Priest, at the end of his remarkably verbose epic of Chauntecleer, solemnly addresses his audience:

> Lo, swich it is for to be recchelees
> And necligent, and truste on flaterye.
> But ye that holden this tale a folye,
> As of a fox, or of a cok and hen,
> Taketh the moralitee, goode men.
> (B² 3736-40)

He then goes on to quote St Paul in a way that suggests that doctrine is produced every time a pen inscribes words on paper—a thought most comforting to an author hard put to determine his own meaning. With Pauline authority on his side, the Nun's Priest exhorts us:

> Taketh the fruit, and lat the chaf be stille.
> (B² 3443)

Now all this certainly bids us find a simple moral in the story; but, so far as I know, no two critics have ever found the same moral: most agree only in rejecting the Nun's Priest's stated moral about negligence and flattery. The reason for this disagreement is, as I have tried to suggest elsewhere, that the real moral of the Tale is in the chaff—the rhetorical amplifications which make of Chauntecleer a good representative of western man trying to maintain his precarious dignity in the face of a universe and of a basic avian (or human) nature which fail to co-operate with him. But the Nun's Priest, characteristically, suggests this moral only by pointing towards another which satisfies nobody.

Another Canterbury narrator, the Knight, similarly asks us to take a simple view of a story which is really very complex. After describing the languishing of Arcite in Theban exile and of Palamon in Athenian prison, both of them quite out of the running in their race for Emily, the narrator finishes off the first part of his poem with a *demande d'amour*:

> You loveres axe I now this questioun:
> Who hath the worse, Arcite or Palamoun?
> (A 1347-8)

With this tidy rhetorical flourish the Knight suggests that his story is a simple one about a rivalry in love. The question invites the reader to take sides in this rivalry, to feel sorrier for one youth than the other, and hence to choose a favourite for the contest that is to come. He appeals, that is, to our sense of justice. Until recently, the majority of Chaucerian critics put their money on Palamon; and since at the end of the story Providence accords him Emily and lets him live happily ever after, while it buries Arcite, this majority have naturally felt that justice has operated in an exemplary manner, and nothing is pleasanter than to see justice behave itself. Yet there has always been a noisy group—with whom I deeply sympathize—who feel that Arcite is very badly treated by the story. This disagreement represents a kind of protracted response to the Knight's rhetorical question.

The lack of critical agreement, however, once again suggests that there is something wrong both about the question and about the debate. If intelligent readers cannot agree on which of the two young men is the more deserving, then there is probably not much difference between them. And indeed, the way the poem carefully balances their claims bears this out. On temperamental grounds you may prefer a man who mistakes his lady for Venus to a man who knows a woman when he sees one, or you may not; but such preference has no moral validity. The poem concerns something larger than the young men's relative deserts, though it is something closely related to that question. Recognition of their equality leads to the conclusion that the poem does not assert the simple triumph of justice when Palamon ends up with Emily, nor the triumph of a malignant anti-justice when Arcite ends up in his cold grave, alone. What it does suggest—and I think with every syllable of its being—is that Providence is not working justly, so far as we can see, when it kills Arcite, nor, so far as we can see, unjustly when it lets Palamon live happily ever after. For no matter how hard we look, we cannot hope to see why Providence behaves as it does; all we can do is our best, making a virtue of necessity, enjoying what is good, and remaining cheerful.

But to most of us this is an unpalatable moral, far less appealing than the one which will result if only we can promote Palamon into an unchallenged position of deserving; and it is a very stale bit of cold cabbage indeed unless it is as hard-won as the Knight's own battles. The experience by which the individual attains the Knight's tempered view of life is an important part of that view, and renders it, if not palatable, digestible and nourishing. This experience must include our questioning of relative values, our desire to discover that even-handed justice does prevail in the universe, and our resistance to the conclusion that justice, so far as we can see, operates at best with only one hand. The emotional history of the ultimate conclusion makes it valid; and the way the Knight's question is framed, pointing at what we should like to believe, and through that at what we shall have to believe, causes us to share in that experience—leads us through the simple to the complex.

It is at the end of *Troilus* that Chaucer, employing the kind of devices I have been discussing, achieves his most complex poetic effect. His narrator has worked hard, from the very beginning, to persuade us of his simplicity, though from the very beginning his simplicity has been compromised by the fact that, apparently unknown to himself, he wavers between two quite different—though equally simple—attitudes towards his story. It is the saddest story in the world, and it is the gladdest story in the world. This double attitude appears strongly in the opening stanzas, when he tells us that his motive for writing is, paradoxically, to bring honour to Love and gladden lovers with a love story so sad that his verses shed tears while he writes them and that Tisiphone is his only appropriate Muse. Yet though he starts out firmly resolved to relate the double sorrow of Troilus

> . . . in loving of Criseide,
> And how that she forsook him er she deide,
> (TC 1.55-6)

as the story progresses he seems to forget all about the second sorrow. The historical perspective, which sees before and after and knows the sad ending, gives way to the limited, immediate view of one who loves the actors in the story, and in his love pines for what is not so desperately that he almost brings it into being. The scholar's motive for telling a sad story simply because it is true finds itself at war with the sentimentalist's motive of telling a love story simply because it is happy and beautiful. The optimism that one acquires when one lives with people so attractive makes a gay future for all seem inevitable. Once launched upon the love story, the narrator refuses to look forward to a future that the scholar in him knows to be already sadly past; at moments when the memory of that sad future breaks in on him, he is likely to deny his own sources, and to suggest that, despite the historical evidence to the contrary, Criseide was, perhaps, not unfaithful at all—men have been lying about her.

For the greater part of the poem the intimately concerned, optimistic narrator is in full control of the story—or rather, the story is in full control of him, and persuades him that a world that has such people in it is not only the best of all possible worlds, but the most possible. When in the fifth book the facts of history force him back towards the historical perspective, which has always known that his happiness and that of the lovers were transitory, illusory, he does his best to resist the implications arising from his ruined story—tries to circumvent them, denies them, slides off them. Thus an extraordinary feeling of tension, even of dislocation, develops from the strife in the narrator's mind between what should be and what was—and hence what is. This tension is the emotional storm-centre which causes the narrator's various shifts and turns in his handling of the ending, and which also determines the great complexity of the poem's ultimate meaning.

So skilfully has Chaucer mirrored his narrator's internal warfare—a kind of nervous breakdown in poetry—that many a critic has concluded that Chaucer himself was bewildered by his poem. One, indeed, roundly condemns the whole fifth book, saying that it reads like 'an earlier draft . . . which its author lacked sufficient interest to revise'. According to this critic, Chaucer 'cannot bring himself to any real enthusiasm for a plot from which the bright lady of his own creation has vanished'. And, elsewhere, 'What had happened to the unhappy Criseyde and to her equally unhappy creator was that the story in which they were involved had betrayed them both'. Now this is, in a rather sad way, the ultimate triumph of Chaucer's method. The critic responds with perfect sympathy to the narrator's bewilderment, even to the extent of seeming to suggest that the poet had written four-fifths of his story before he discovered how it came out. But in fact Chaucer's warmly sympathetic narrator has blinded the critic's eyes as effectively as he had blinded his own. It is not true that the bright lady of Chaucer's creation has vanished—Criseide is still very much present in book five. What has vanished is the bright dream of the enduring power of human love, and in a burst of creative power that it is not easy to match elsewhere.

For the *moralitee* of *Troilus and Criseide* (and by morality I do not mean 'ultimate meaning') is simply this: that human love, and by a sorry corollary everything human, is unstable and illusory. I give the moral so flatly now because in the remainder of this paper I shall be following the narrator in his endeavour to avoid it, and indeed shall be eagerly abetting him in trying to avoid it, and even pushing him away when he finally accepts it. I hope in this way to suggest how Chaucer, by manipulating his narrator, achieves an objective image of the poem's significance that at once greatly qualifies and enhances this moral, and one that is, of course, far more profound and less absolute than my flat-footed statement. The meaning of the poem is not the moral, but a complex qualification of the moral.

Let us turn now to that part of the poem, containing the last eighteen stanzas, which is often referred to by modern scholars, though not by the manuscripts, as the Epilogue. I object to the term because it implies that this passage was tacked on to the poem after the poet had really finished his work, so that it is critically if not physically detachable from what has gone before. And while I must admit that the nature of this passage, its curious twists and turns, its occasional air of fecklessness, set it off from what has gone before, it also seems to me to be the head of the whole body of the poem.

The last intimately observed scene of the action is the final, anticlimactic interview between Troilus and Pandarus, wherein the latter is driven by the sad logic of his loyalty and of his pragmatism to express hatred of his niece, and to wish her dead. Pandarus's last words are, 'I can namore saye', and it is now up to the narrator, who is as heart-broken as Troilus and Pandarus, to express the significance of his story. His first reaction is to take the epic high road; by means of the exalted style to reinvest Troilus with the human dignity that his unhappy love has taken from him. The narrator starts off boldly enough:

> Greet was the sorwe and plainte of Troilus;
> But forth hire cours Fortune ay gan to holde.
> Criseide loveth the sone of Tydeüs,
> And Troilus moot weepe in cares colde.
>
> (TC v. 1744-7)

But though the manner is epic, the subject is not: an Aeneas in Dido's pathetic plight is no fit subject for Virgilian style. And the narrator, overcome by the pathos of his story, takes refuge in moralization:

> Swich is this world, whoso it can biholde:
> In eech estaat is litel hertes reste—
> God leve us for to take it for the beste!

How true! And how supremely, brilliantly, inadequate! It has been said that all experience does no more than prove some platitude or other, but one hopes that poetic experience will do more, or in any case that poetry will not go from pathos to bathos. This moral, the trite moral of the Monk's Tale— Isn't life awful?—which the Monk arrives at—again and again—*a priori* would be accepted by many a medieval man as a worthy moral for the *Troilus*, and the narrator is a medieval man. But the poet behind the narrator is aware that an experience that has been intimately shared—not merely viewed historically, as are the Monk's tragedies—requires not a moral, but a meaning arrived at *a posteriori*, something earned, and in a sense new. Moreover, the narrator seems still to be asking the question, Can nothing be salvaged from the wreck of the story? For he goes on once more to have recourse to epic enhancement of his hero, more successfully this time, since it is the martial heroism of Troilus, rather than his unhappy love, that is the subject: there follow two militant stanzas recounting his prowess and his encounters with Diomede. But again the epic impulse fails, for the narrator's real subject is not war but unhappy love, for which epic values will still do nothing—will neither salvage the dignity of Troilus nor endow his experience with meaning. In a wistful stanza, the narrator faces his failure to do by epic style what he desires to have done:

> And if I hadde ytaken for to write
> The armes of this ilke worthy man,
>     [But, unfortunately, *arma virumque non cano*]
> Than wolde ich of his batailes endite;
> But for that I to writen first bigan
> Of his love, I have said as I can—
> His worthy deedes, whoso list hem heere,
> Rede Dares—he can telle hem alle yfere.
>
> (1765-71)

This sudden turn from objective description to introspection mirrors the narrator's quandary. Unable to get out of his hopeless predicament, he does what we all tend to do when we are similarly placed: he begins to wonder why he ever got himself into it. The sequel of this unprofitable speculation is likely to be panic, and the narrator very nearly panics when he sees staring him in the face another possible moral for the love poem he has somehow been unwise enough to recite. The moral that is staring him in the face is written in the faces of the ladies of his audience, the anti-feminist moral which is at once obvious and, from a court poet, unacceptable:

> Biseeching every lady bright of hewe,
> And every gentil womman what she be,
> That al be that Criseide was untrewe,
> That for that gilt she nat be wroth with me.
> Ye may hir giltes in othere bookes see;
> And gladlier I wol write, if you leste,
> Penelopeës trouthe and good Alceste.

While anticipating the ladies' objections, the narrator has, with that relief only a true coward can appreciate, glimpsed a possible way out: denial of responsibility for what the poem says. He didn't write it in the first place, it has nothing to do with him, and anyhow he would much rather have written about faithful women. These excuses are, of course, very much in the comic mood of the Prologue to the *Legend of Good Women* where Alceste, about whom he would prefer to have written, defends him from Love's wrath on the grounds that, being no more than a translator, he wrote about Criseide 'from innocence, and knew not what he said'. And if he can acquit himself of responsibility for Criseide by pleading permanent inanity, there is no reason why he cannot get rid of all his present tensions by funnelling them into a joke against himself. This he tries to do by turning upside down the anti-feminist moral of the story:

> N'l saye nat this al only for thise men,
> But most for wommen that bitraised be . . .

And I haven't recited this exclusively for men, but also, or rather but mostly, for women who are betrayed

> Thrugh false folk—God yive hem sorwe, amen!—
> That with hir grete wit and subtiltee
> Bitraise you; and this commeveth me
> To speke, and in effect you alle I praye,
> Beeth war of men, and herkneth what I saye.

The last excursion into farce—in a poem that contains a good deal of farce—is this outrageous inversion of morals, which even so has a grotesque relevance if all human love, both male and female, is in the end to be adjudged unstable. With the narrator's recourse to comedy the poem threatens to end. At any rate, he asks it to go away:

> Go, litel book, go, litel myn tragedye,
> Ther God thy makere yit, er that he die,
> So sende might to make in som comedye. . . .

(Presumably a comedy will not blow up in his face as this story has, and will let him end on a note like the one he has just sounded.) There follows the celebrated injunction of the poet to his book not to vie with other poetry, but humbly to kiss the steps of Virgil, Ovid, Homer, Lucan, and Statius. This is the modesty convention again, but transmuted, I believe, into something close to arrogance. Perhaps the poem is not to be classed with the works of these great poets, but I do not feel that the narrator succeeds in belittling his work by mentioning it in connection with them; there is such a thing as inviting comparison by eschewing comparison. It seems that the narrator has abandoned his joke, and is taking his 'little book'—of more than 8,000 lines—seriously. Increasing gravity characterizes the next stanza, which begins with the hope that the text will not be miswritten nor mismetred by scribes and lesser breeds without the law of final -e. Then come two lines of emphatic prayer:

> And red wherso thou be, or elles songe,
> That thou be understonde, God I biseeche.

It is perhaps inconsiderate of the narrator to implore us to take his sense when he has been so irresolute about defining his sense. But the movement of the verse now becomes sure and strong, instead of uncertain and aimless, as the narrator moves confidently towards a meaning.

For in the next stanza, Troilus meets his death. This begins—once again—in the epic style, with perhaps a glance at the *Iliad*:

> The wratthe, as I bigan you for to saye,
> Of Troilus the Greekes boughten dere.

Such dignity as the high style can give is thus, for the last time, proffered Troilus. But for him there is to be no last great battle in the West, and both the stanza, and Troilus's life, end in pathos:

> But wailaway, save only Goddes wille:
> Despitously him slow the fierse Achille.

Troilus's spirit at once ascends into the upper spheres whence he looks down upon this little earth and holds all vanity as compared with the full felicity of heaven. The three stanzas describing Troilus's afterlife afford him that reward which medieval Christianity allowed to the righteous heathen. And in so doing, they salvage from the human wreck of the story the human qualities of

Troilus that are of enduring value—most notably, his *trouthe*, the integrity for which he is distinguished. Moreover, this recognition by the plot that some human values transcend human life seems to enable the narrator to come to a definition of the poem's meaning which he has hitherto been unwilling to make. Still close to his characters, he witnesses Troilus's rejection of earthly values, and then, apparently satisfied, now that the mortal good in Troilus has been given immortal reward, he is willing to make that rejection of *all* mortal goods towards which the poem has, despite his resistance, been driving him. His rejection occurs—most unexpectedly—in the third of these stanzas. Troilus, gazing down at the earth and laughing within himself at those who mourn his death,

> . . . dampned al oure werk that folweth so
> The blinde lust, the which that may nat laste,
> And sholden al oure herte on hevene caste.

Up until the last line Troilus has been the subject of every main verb in the entire passage; but after he has damned all *our* work, by one of those syntactical ellipses that make Middle English so fluid a language, Troilus's thought is extended to include both narrator and reader: in the last line, *And sholden al oure herte on hevene caste*, the plural verb *sholden* requires the subject *we*; but this subject is omitted, because to the narrator the sequence of the sense is, at last, overpoweringly clear. When, after all his attempts not to have to reject the values inherent in his love story, he finally does reject them, he does so with breath-taking ease.

He does so, indeed, with dangerous ease. Having taken up arms against the world and the flesh, he lays on with a will:

> Swich fin hath, lo, this Troilus for love;
> Swich fin hath al his grete worthinesse;
> Swich fin hath his estaat real above;
> Swich fin his lust, swich fin hath his noblesse;
> Swich fin hath false worldes brotelnesse:
> And thus bigan his loving of Criseide,
> As I have told, and in this wise he deide.

But impressive as this stanza is, its movement is curious. The first five lines express, with increasing force, disgust for a world in which everything—not only what merely *seems* good, but also what really *is* good—comes to nothing in the end. Yet the last two lines,

> And thus bigan his loving of Criseide,
> As I have told, and in this wise he deide,

have, I think, a sweetness of tone that contrasts strangely with the emphatic disgust that precedes them. They seem to express a deep sadness for a doomed potential—as if the narrator, while forced by the evidence to condemn everything his poem has stood for, cannot really quite believe that it has come to nothing. The whole lovely aspiration of the previous action is momentarily recreated in the spare summary of this couplet.

The sweetness of tone carries over into the next two stanzas, the much-quoted ones beginning

> O yonge, freshe folkes, he or she,
> In which that love up groweth with youre age,
> Repaireth hoom fro worldly vanitee,
> And of youre herte up casteth the visage
> To thilke God that after his image
> You made; and thinketh al nis but a faire
> This world that passeth soone as flowres faire.

The sweetness here adheres not only to what is being rejected, but also to what is being sought in its stead, and this marks a development in the narrator. For he does not now seem so much to be fleeing away, in despair and disgust, from an ugly world—the world of the Monk's Tale—as he seems to be moving voluntarily through this world *towards* something infinitely better. And while this world is a wretched one—ultimately—in which all love is *feined*, 'pretended' and 'shirked', it is also a world full of the young potential of human love—'In which that love up groweth with *oure* age'; a world which, while it passes soon, passes soon as flowers fair. All the illusory loveliness of a world which is man's only reality is expressed in the very lines that reject that loveliness.

In these stanzas the narrator has been brought to the most mature and complex expression of what is involved in the Christian rejection of the world that seems to be, and indeed is, man's home, even though he knows there is a better one. But the narrator himself remains dedicated to simplicity, and makes one last effort to resolve the tension in his mind between loving a world he ought to hate and hating a world he cannot help loving; he endeavours to root out the love:

> Lo, here of payens cursed olde rites;
> Lo, here what alle hir goddes may availe;
> Lo, here thise wrecched worldes appetites;
> Lo, here the fin and guerdon for travaile
> Of Jove, Appollo, of Mars, of swich rascaile;
> Lo, here the forme of olde clerkes speeche
> In poetrye, if ye hir bookes seeche.

For the second time within a few stanzas a couplet has undone the work of the five lines preceding it. In them is harsh, excessively harsh, condemnation of the world of the poem, including gods and rites that have played no great part in it. In brilliant contrast to the tone of these lines is the exhausted calm of the last two:

> Lo, here the forme of olde clerkes speeche
> In poetrye, if ye hir bookes seeche.

There is a large imprecision about the point of reference of this couplet. I do not know whether its *Lo here* refers to the five preceding lines or to the poem as a whole, but I suppose it refers to the poem as a whole, as the other four *Lo here's* do. If this is so, then the form of *olde clerkes speeche* is being damned as well as the *payens cursed olde rites*—by parataxis, at least. Yet it is not, for the couplet lacks the heavy, fussy indignation of the earlier lines: instead of indignation there is, indeed, dignity. I suggest that the couplet once more reasserts, in its simplicity, all the implicit and explicit human values that the poem has dealt with, even though these are, to a medieval Christian, ultimately insignificant. The form of old clerks' speech in poetry is the sad story that human history tells. It is sad, it is true, it is lovely, and it is significant, for it is poetry.

This is the last but one of the narrator's searches for a resolution for his poem. I have tried to show how at the end of *Troilus* Chaucer has manipulated a narrator capable of only a simple view of reality in such a way as to achieve the poetic expression of an extraordinarily complex one. The narrator, moved by his simple devotion to Troilus, to Pandarus, above all to Criseide, has been vastly reluctant to find that their story, so full of the illusion of happiness, comes to nothing—that the potential of humanity comes to nothing. To avoid this—seemingly simple—conclusion he has done everything he could. He has tried the epic high road; he has tried the broad highway of trite moralization; he has tried to eschew responsibility; he has tried to turn it all into a joke; and all these devices have failed. Finally, with every other means of egress closed, he has subscribed to Troilus's rejection of his own story, though only when, like Gregory when he wept for Trajan, he has seen his desire for his hero's salvation confirmed. Once having made the rejection, he has thrown himself into world-hating with enthusiasm. But now the counterbalance asserts its power. For the same strong love of the world of his story that prevented him from reaching the Christian rejection permeates and qualifies his expression of the rejection. Having painfully climbed close to the top of the ridge he did not want to climb, he cannot help looking back with longing at the darkening but still fair valley in which he lived; and every resolute thrust forward ends with a glance backward. In having his narrator behave thus, Chaucer has achieved a meaning only great poetry can achieve. The world he knows and the heaven he believes in grow ever farther and farther apart as the woeful contrast between them is developed, and even closer and closer together as the narrator blindly unites them in the common bond of his love. Every false start he has made has amounted, not to a negative, but to a positive; has been a necessary part of the experience without which the moral of the poem would be as meaningless and unprofitable as in the form I gave it a little while ago. The poem states, what much of Chaucer's poetry states, the necessity under which men lie of living in, making the best of, enjoying, and loving a world from which they must remain detached and which they must ultimately hate: a little spot of earth that with the sea embracéd is, as in Book Three Criseide was embraced by Troilus.

For this paradox there is no logical resolution. In the last two stanzas of the poem Chaucer, after asking Gower and Strode for correction, invokes the power that, being supra-logical itself, can alone resolve paradox. He echoes Dante's mighty prayer to the Trinity, 'that al maist circumscrive', and concludes with the lines:

> So make us, Jesus, for thy mercy digne,
> For love of Maide and Moder thyn benigne.

The poem has concerned a mortal woman whose power to love failed, and it ends with the one mortal woman whose power to love is everlasting. I think it is significant that the prayer of the poem's ending leads up, not to Christ, son of God, but to his mother, daughter of Eve—towards heaven, indeed, but towards heaven through human experience.

E. TALBOT DONALDSON

# The Effect of the "Merchant's Tale"

Ｏne of the most profound and per-
haps most significant of the recent disagreements among Chaucerians concerns the tone of the Merchant's Tale. Is this story, as Tatlock and many of
the older critics have held, a dark one, filled with bitterness and disgust for the
human race as represented by January and May and Damian? Or is it, as
several recent writers believe, a merry jest, the humour of which is entirely
characteristic of the fabliau genre—something that will, as one critic supposes, make us 'glad'? Some years ago at approximately the same time that
Professor Bronson was lightly dismissing the tale as just 'another high card in
the unending Game between the Sexes', another Chaucerian was writing
that in it 'the dam has given way, and the ugly muck that formerly lay hidden
beneath the surface'—presumably of the Merchant's personality—'is exposed to the sight of all'. While this is obviously an overstatement, as well as
an overwrought statement, I continue to believe in its sense, even though I
now deplore the rankness of its rhetorical colouring. Faced with two such
divergent opinions, the student who had never read Chaucer but only
Chaucerians—dreary fate—might well conclude that Professor Bronson and
I were talking about different stories, or else that one or both of us had not
read the Merchant's Tale very well if at all.

This kind of divergency of opinion is doubtless due to our both writing
descriptive criticism, which means that while we both pretend to be describing the tale objectively, we are in fact describing our reactions to it: we are
casting on its persons and incidents a kind of spotlight, to be sure, but one
that takes its colouring from our own preconceptions, and these neither of us
has troubled to justify to the reader. Thus Professor Bronson succeeds in
making everything about the tale sound extremely funny, although he admits

From *Speaking of Chaucer*. Copyright © 1970, 1977 by E. Talbot Donaldson. W. W.
Norton & Co., 1970.

that it takes on a certain amount of bitterness because of the characterization of its narrator as an extremely bilious, misogynistic man. On the other hand, I make the same things sound very grim indeed, although I am careful to say, if not to show, that they are somehow very funny. In this paper I should like to try better to justify my feeling that the Merchant's Tale is in truth a grim thing by examining some of the passages that form the basis for my feeling.

First let me try to chase away two red herrings that are constantly stealing the bait from those who fish for literary values in the murky waters of this particular narrative. The first is the general problem of the comic as opposed to the serious in literature. Every one is, of course, aware that the fact that a literary work is funny does not rule out its being highly serious—does not rule out its being, sometimes, as profound a commentary on human life as the most overt tragedy. To put it briefly, laughter is not by necessity thoughtless. I have to repeat this truism because any one who tries to emphasize the darker side of a humorous tale becomes a ready victim of the quick *ad hominem* rebuttal which blurs the distinction between *serious* meaning 'solemn' and *serious* meaning 'important'. 'Ho, ho, ho', the opposition chortles, 'the poor fellow doesn't realize that it's all just a joke'—and, of course, to be caught missing a joke is to forfeit one's respectability as a critic: I'm afraid many of us have been guilty at one time or another of demonstrating our critical superiority by finding jokes in Chaucer's text that our opponents have missed—sometimes, indeed, jokes that Chaucer himself may have missed. But I hope in this paper I may be allowed to talk about the Merchant's Tale without being unduly self-conscious that I am neglecting the obvious fact that it is very funny, in a sad sort of way. In return, I shall apologize to the critic whom I cited rather derisively as having said that the tale is one that will make us glad; any profound work of literature makes one glad, and I am as glad of the Merchant's Tale as he—though not, I confess, immediately after I have finished reading it, when my feeling is aptly expressed by the Host: 'Ey, Goddes mercy!'

The second point needing preliminary discussion is more limited in scope. Only twenty-three of the fifty-two MSS containing the Merchant's Tale include the Merchant's Prologue, in which the Merchant is characterized (for the first time) as an embittered bridegroom. This has led to a good deal of speculation about Chaucer's original intention with regard to the tale, and provides Professor Bronson with one of the bases for his argument that Chaucer wrote it not for a bilious Merchant, but to be told *in propria persona*, from his own mouth, whence it would presumably have come with merry humour devoid of bitterness. Yet when MSS offer several alternatives, one of which characterizes a narrator in a way appropriate to the tale while the others either adapt a link universally admitted to have been written by

Chaucer for some one else (in this case, the Franklin) or else make no advance assignment at all, it is only common sense to assume that the more satisfactory alternative represents Chaucer's intention. The frequent absence of the Merchant's Prologue from the MSS may indeed suggest the possibility that Chaucer added it to an already completed (and circulated) tale, but it by no means establishes a probability that he did so: we simply do not know enough about the early history of the copying of the *Canterbury Tales* to feel secure in the belief that the absence of the Merchant's Prologue represents a genuine authorial variant as opposed to a mere scribal one. And even if the variant does represent an earlier phase of authorial intention, since it is clear that Chaucer wrote the appropriate Merchant's Prologue that is preserved in twenty-three MSS, then the variant is important only to a study of Chaucer's method of composition and not to the criticism of the Merchant's Tale as it now stands. Only if, as a literary fact, the tale failed to fit the narrator as he is characterized in its prologue would the existence of other MS alternatives to the prologue become significant, and only provided that among these alternatives was a more satisfactory reading. But not even Professor Bronson denies the suitability of the Merchant's Tale to the Merchant as he is characterized in what is an undeniably authentic prologue. He merely seems to regret it because of the preconceptions he entertains about the kind of poetry that witty, urbane, genial Chaucer ought to have written.

Specifically, he believes that the assignment of the tale to the Merchant, as well as the composition of the Merchant's Prologue (admittedly an unexpected but surely not impossible extension of his portrait in the General Prologue) took place well after the composition of the tale itself. Here is Professor Bronson's statement of the consequences of his belief:

> . . . what the poet may not at once have realized is that the explanation he had provided [that is, the Merchant's Prologue] worked an instant sea-change on the story itself. The Merchant's misogyny impregnated the whole piece with a mordant venom, inflaming what originally had been created for the sake of mirth. That Chaucer could have foreseen this effect is very unlikely.

It is not unfair to say that a good deal more bitterness has been let into the Merchant's Tale by this paragraph, which is near the end of Professor Bronson's article, than one would have expected from his earlier argument. And I will surely allow the point that the 'Merchant's misogyny impregnate[s] the whole piece with a mordant venom'—obviously, that's why the misogyny has been so lovingly presented in the Merchant's Prologue. But since I do not believe in art by inadvertence, I cannot see how Chaucer could not have been aware of what would happen when he assigned a certain kind of tale to a certain kind of narrator: he was after all a master of the art of manipulating and multiplying fictional contexts. But even though I cannot help gasping at Professor Bronson's wholly unsupported (and unsupportable) statement that it is 'unlikely' that Chaucer foresaw the effect he in fact achieved, it is not my present purpose to defend the poet from inexplicable slanders on his artistic intelligence. What I wish to do is to show that it is idle to speculate, in a complete absence of respectable evidence, about when Chaucer did what with the Merchant's Tale, since it is a literary fact that it is an intensely bitter story, which, while it suits perfectly its intensely bitter narrator, would of itself, even if it had never been assigned to a specific Canterbury pilgrim, have characterized its narrator as one whose vision was limited almost exclusively to the dark side of things.

The most obvious feature of the Merchant's Tale is its juxtaposition of the seemingly, or potentially, beautiful with the unmistakably ugly, of the 'faire, fresshe' May with the 'olde' January. This juxtaposition of beautiful and ugly is not static but dynamic, for the ugly constantly casts its shadow over the beautiful or, conversely, the seemingly beautiful ultimately reveals itself to be as ugly, in its own way, as that with which it is juxtaposed. Moreover, the main juxtaposition is reflected in all the story's incidents and throughout the details of its poetic style. If I may use a somewhat metaphysical metaphor, the central situation of the story is like the sun suffering eclipse: during a solar eclipse, every bright patch of sunlight screened through a natural filter such as foliage at each moment exactly reproduces the phase of the sun's darkening, so that the ground under leafy trees is covered with hundreds of tiny eclipses, and every sunny spot suffers the encroachment of the shadow. And everywhere within the tale the shadow encroaches. The narrator's (and narrative's) bitterness is such that it goes beyond the inevitable anti-Platonism of the selfish disillusioned romanticist almost to a complete denial of the possibility of any human value: not only is what is beautiful, and hence what one wants to believe good, actually ugly, but even those things that are generally accepted unquestioningly as valuable are either made to seem fatally flawed or are tainted by the Merchant's poison.

The central juxtaposition and its myriad concomitant reflections are handled with what might be called perfectly bad taste. I'm not sure that this isn't just as difficult an artistic effect to achieve as perfectly good taste, for it often consists, not of a piling up of vulgarities, but of the introduction into a relatively innocuous passage of a single, carefully selected vulgarity that will produce an aesthetic shock upon the reader, destroying a context which seemed fair, or one which he at least wanted to believe was fair. The poem is thus constantly affronting our aesthetic sense, bringing our emotions into play in such a way as to confuse our moral judgment, which finds no safe place to settle. The distinctive tone of the Merchant's Tale becomes clear when one compares it, in plot summary, with the Miller's: two succulent young females, May and Alison, married to two variants of the type *senex amans*, January and John, and assorted would-be lovers; and, in the plot summary, two vulgar climaxes, with the Miller's potentially more shocking to the reader than the Merchant's. Yet the drunken Miller has in his own way perfect taste, and his narration of a most vulgar event, Absolon's kissing of Alison's rump, is done with a kind of high-poetic awe—almost as if he were exclaiming, 'What hath God wrought?'—that at once heightens the comedy and diminishes offensiveness. On the other hand, the Merchant, excusing with a mealy apology the baldness of his language, succeeds in making a long-anticipated act of coition seem extremely shocking.

'Healthy animality': I detest the patronizing term, but can't think of a better one to describe the Miller's Tale in its relation to the Merchant's, to which one may apply the modification, 'mere bestiality'. Notice the following lines, January's prospectus for a wife:

> 'I wol noon old wif han in no manere;
> She shal nat passe sixteen yeer certain—
> Old fissh and yong flessh wol I have fain.
> Bet is,' quod he, 'a pik than a pikerel,
> And bet than old boef is the tendre veel:
> I wol no womman thritty yeer of age—
> It is but bene-straw and greet forage.'
>                                          (E1416-22)

Here January, in the guise of a gourmet who knows all about *la bonne cuisine* whether fish, flesh, or female, is already, if unwittingly, seeing his future wife as the young beast he actually gets. And, as so often happens in the tale, the images the speaker uses catch him up in their own truth. Thus in the last line, the *beanstraw* and *great forage* are, of course, foods not for a *bon vivant*, but for what he is unconsciously admitting himself to be: that is, they are coarse, dry fodder for an old beast stable-bound by winter, which is what January is despite his colt's tooth. And even that fish is going to catch up with him later, when he is described making love to May:

> He lulleth hire, he kisseth hire ful ofte—
> With thikke bristles of his beerd unsofte,
> Lik to the skin of houndfissh, sharpe as brere,
> For he was shave al newe in his manere.
>                                          (E1823-6)

Old fish, ineptly razored, painfully embracing tender veal.

There is no need to labour the matter of Chaucer's careful portrayal of the uglier side of the central juxtaposition. This is made rank enough seriously to effect the quality, if not the quantity, of our laughter. Rather more subtle is his handling of that bright beast May. Initially she seems a sort of Galatea created in response to the fantasies of January; but despite the reckless assumption of the aged Pygmalion, the statue when it finally comes to life has no internal qualities to match its outward loveliness. Of course, revelation of what May's qualities really are is postponed as long as possible. Meanwhile the Merchant associates with her—though he does not actually ascribe to her—such thoughts as the romanticist might think she ought to have: he manages to convey without an overt assertion her disgust with January's love-making; and when Damian becomes love-sick for her, the Merchant assures him in a rhetorical outburst that he can never attain her—'She wol alway saye nay'. But finally, on her visit to the squire, May allows him to thrust his letter into her hand, and she hides it in her bosom—her first genuine action in the poem. Thereafter the Merchant relates, with superbly bad taste, how, upon her return to January,

> She feined hire as that she moste goon
> Ther as ye woot that every wight hath neede,
> And whan she of this bille hath taken heede,
> She rente it al to cloutes at the laste,
> And in the privee softely it caste.
>                                                   (E1950-4)

In the word *softely* and the object with which it is juxtaposed is the climax of Chaucer's treatment of May, and the microcosm of his treatment of things throughout the poem as a whole. *Softly* had in Middle English as it still has a range of meanings entirely appropriate to May's literal action, 'quietly, surreptitiously', and in this respect it is straightforwardly realistic. But *softly* also has, and cannot help having, another range of meanings that associate it with warm weather, warm May, tender, gentle, alluring womanhood, femininity at its most romantically attractive; and thus the sense of the lines moves backward and forward between May's beauty, May's deceit, and the privy.

May is, however, alone within the poem in being allowed to remain for any length of time unsullied, and the fact that everything else is sullied makes her descent seem inevitable even while it is shocking. Indeed, if the narrative had turned suddenly, at a point about halfway to the ending, from the beautiful to the ugly, it might come closer to being the outrageous jest that readers like Professor Bronson want it to be, for a really sudden shock—like Thomas's gift to the Friar in the Summoner's Tale—is likely to turn realism into fantasy. But the poem has been infected with venom from the very beginning, a venom compounded in part of a most cynical kind of realism. And this venom is no mere overflow from the initial characterization of the Merchant-narrator, but part of the tale's pigmentation. Let us look for a moment at the passage that has been called Chaucer's most daring—or most rash—use of irony. The poem begins with a quick sketch of the bachelor-lecher who in his old age has determined to marry—'were it for holinesse or for dotage I can nat saye':

> 'Noon other lif,' saide he, 'is worth a bene,
> For wedlok is so esy and so clene
> That in this world it is a Paradis.'
> Thus saide this olde knight that was so wis.
> (E1263-6)

After that last line, which is as near to a sneer as poetry can come, the narrator intrudes to say:

> And certainly, as sooth as God is king,
> To take a wif, it is a glorious thing,
> And namely whan a man is old and hoor.
> (E1267-9)

These lines introduce a 126-line passage in which everything that might be said in favour of marriage gets itself said, and a good deal more. Readers have often observed that this passage has nothing in it to show that it is ironical beyond its context, and some have even described it as a perfectly straightforward exposition of the medieval ideals of marriage. But Professor Bronson is right in noting that its sense, whatever its context, is absurd. Indeed, it represents a kind of double distortion of reality: a rebuttal of antifeminism erected on the same bases as antifeminism. According to Jerome, who despite being a saint was not on this subject either clear-headed or fair-minded, the sole motive of a wife is to frustrate her husband. In the Merchant's panegyric, this simple formula is turned upside down with an equally simple-minded result: the sole motive of a wife is to assure her husband's comfort. Both opinions rest on the basic assumption that women were really created to be servile beasts, though according to one they reject their assigned role and according to the other they accept it gratefully. The masculine selfishness latent in the whole antifeminist tradition reaches its clearest expression in the Merchant's praise of matrimony: not 'he for God only, she for God in him', but he for himself, she for him. It is foolish though understandable to suppose, as January did, that May's beauty implies some special virtue, but it is simply absurd to suppose that wives will love their husbands just because they were kind enough to purchase them.

And not even this panegyric is allowed to bask uninterruptedly in the bright sunlight of its own vacuity: the shadow of bitterness falls here too, and in a rather surprising place. Following his source, which is either Chaucer's own *Melibeus* or its source, Albertano's endless *Book of Counsel*, the Merchant adduces the creation of Eve in order to establish for his hearers woman's usefulness to man:

> And herke why I saye nat this for nought
> That womman is for mannes help ywrought:
> The hye God, whan he hadde Adam maked,
> And sawgh him allone, bely-naked,
> God of his grete goodnesse saide than,
> 'Lat us now make an help unto this man
> Lik to himself.' And than he made him Eve.
>                                                 (E1323-9)

I am unable to read this passage without feeling that in making Eve the Creator is motivated more by a kind of cynical pity than by love for what He has made. The clue to this feeling is that the narrator has substituted for God's statement, 'It is not good for a man to be alone', the action of God's looking at the poor naked thing and seeming to draw from Adam's appearance the conclusion that he had better have some help—there is no *imago Dei* here. 'And sawgh him allone, bely-naked.' Belly-naked is one of those phrases that offer pitfalls to the unwary. In my youth boys used to use it for the way they went swimming when there was no one to see; but it was evidently considered a vulgar phrase, for I don't believe we would have used it before our mothers, or not unscathed in any case; indeed, the word *belly* in any usage was so frowned upon that one still hears the euphemism *tummy* from the mouths of otherwise highly sophisticated speakers. But of course we have all been taught that those good old Anglo-Saxon words—and *belly* is from an Anglo-Saxon word meaning 'bag'—were commonly used in the Middle Ages, and that the vulgarity we associate with them is of relatively recent development. And surely this is sometimes so, but not so often as we think, and not, I think, in the present case. Chaucer only uses *belly* meaning 'stomach' three times in all his works. One of these is in the brilliantly vulgar context of the Summoner's Tale, where it is referred to the highly gaseous churl who is to provide the gift that may be divided equally among thirteen friars. The other is in the Pardoner's sermon, a splendid example of what might be called homiletic shock-treatment, or Pauline hortatory vulgarity. For St Paul is, of course, the great original:

> O wombe, O bely, O stinking cod,
> Fulfilled of dong and of corrupcioun!
> At either ende of thee foul is the soun.
>                                                 (C534-6)

It seems a reasonable supposition that if Chaucer had not meant to have his narrator vulgarize the creation of Adam and Eve he would have chosen another term than *bely-naked*. 'And God saw Adam alone, belly-naked; and then of his great goodness he said, " et us now make an help unto this man—like to himself". And then he made him Eve.' And Eve, another poor worm, is as like Adam as May turns out to be like January. It is a depressing thought.

This sour note, which sounds so often in the poem as to be characteristic of it, sounds again in the wedding of January and May, even more unharmoniously than it does in the Creation. Of course, one is fully aware that no marriage ceremony should be taking place between this ill-matched couple—that January is disobeying Cato's and Nature's precept that man should wed only his similitude. But the marriage ceremony itself is not responsible: it is not its fault that the bride and groom are unsuited, and it remains a 'ful greet sacrament'. Yet the narrator's 'mordant venom'—to borrow Professor Bronson's phrase again—sullies the ritual because he hates the participants:

> Forth comth the preest with stole aboute his nekke,
> And bad hire be lik Sarra and Rebekke
> In wisdom and in trouthe of mariage,
> And saide his orisons as is usage,
> And croucheth hem, and bad God sholde hem blesse,
> And made al siker ynough with holinesse.
>
> (E1703-08)

This passage—Mendelssohn on a flat piano—contains at least two dissonances that are worth examining. One is the repetition of the verb *bidden* (*bad*), used first in the sense 'command'—he commanded her to be like Sarah and Rebecca—and then in the sense 'pray'—he prayed that God would bless them. That is, 'pray' is the expected sense, but I can never read the passage without feeling that the second use of *bad* has been infected by the first, so that what the words really are saying is, 'And the priest told God to bless 'em'. The phrasing seems abruptly jussive. Indeed, my second translation, while idiomatic, is literally accurate. Moreover, there is some reason for making it, at least as a simultaneous alternate. In Chaucer's works the verb *bidden* occurs 124 times: 104 times it clearly means 'command', and only in twenty uses is the meaning 'pray' either requisite or probable. It occurs just six times with God as the object (*bidden God*), and in the other five the syntax is such as to make it clear that the bidder is making a request of God, not giving Him an order. But here the syntax is bald: 'bad God sholde'. This construction seems to me to reflect the disgusted disillusion of the narrator, who here reduces, with a contempt bred of familiarity, Christian ritual to perfunctory hocus-pocus. The priest is seen as a kind of witch-doctor who presumably controls the Almighty much as Prospero controls Caliban. He dispenses holiness as if it were some sort of magic powder that he can scatter around in order to secure the marriage—an insecticide to ward off the flies of evil. But we know his magic isn't going to work. And that associations with primitive magic are what Chaucer had in mind as he wrote the lines is suggested by something else: when the priest makes the sign of the cross over the bride and groom, the verb used for the action is *crouchen*: 'And croucheth hem'. This Middle English word, common enough to have become part of the name of a whole order of friars, apparently had low associations for Chaucer: the only other time it occurs in his works is in the Miller's Tale, just before old John recites his ancient night-spell. Shaking Nicholas out of his assumed trance, John exclaims,

> I crouche thee from elves and fro wightes!
> (A3479)

Here, too, the background is one of primitive magic.

It is this recurrent action of derogating things-as-they-are, especially those things that we instinctively place value on, that imparts to the Merchant's Tale its large content of emotional energy. And when one's emotions are being constantly stirred up, one cannot read with detachment—cannot remain uninvolved. The Shipman's Tale, another study of opportunistic sexual behaviour marital and extramarital, produces an entirely different effect, because no grain of genuine emotion ever scratches its smooth, glassy surface. Even the Reeve's Tale, a vindictive story told by an angry man, evokes from all but the most squeamish nothing but laughter: the fact that the Reeve believes all millers to be thieves has not jaundiced his view of life as a whole, and under his cool direction the fabliau-machine works effortlessly to show that proud, thieving bullies get their just deserts. But the Merchant's hard-earned conviction that wives are inevitably and triumphantly deceitful and unfaithful so infects his depiction of the world that the reader is made, willy-nilly, to suffer some measure of pity and terror. It is easy enough to laugh at futile, inarticulate wrath, as the pilgrims laugh at the Pardoner when the Host's insult reduces him to silence; but an articulate wrath that keeps wounding our sensibilities necessarily involves us in itself. Detachment only comes to the reader of the Merchant's Tale at the very end with the culminating outrage, which is an incident of such high and horrible fantasy that it disconnects us from our sense of reality. Yet this detachment comes too late to alter the experience that has gone before, and has, indeed, the paradoxical effect of enhancing its dark values. When May climbs the tree over January's stooping back—tender youth over stooping age—we have to surrender to laughter, but not without some of that sense of sadness we feel when what we have been emotionally involved with moves beyond the point where we can any longer care.

In the meanwhile, between the wedding and the climax there takes place a shift in the emotional balance of the two units in the tale's central juxtaposition. Our natural sympathy for May, evoked by her physical loveliness, and our natural disgust with January reach their respective climaxes in the Merchant's description of their wedding night. Professor Bronson tells us that the mismating of youth and age 'was not the kind of problem that [Chaucer's] generation worried over', but at least one member of his generation, William Langland in *Piers Plowman*, worried over it rather eloquently, and it seems to me that Chaucer took some trouble to make the reader of the Merchant's Tale worry over it when he quietly shifted the point of view of the narrative so that we see the wedding night through May's eyes rather than January's. But later, when May's female resourcefulness begins to work, some of the disgust we felt for January begins to spill over into our feeling for May: the eclipse is becoming total. And when January goes blind, some of the sympathy we felt for May is displaced and spills over into our feeling for him. Morally, of course, there is little to choose, nor has there been any real exchange of roles, for January is as bad as ever and May is merely revealing herself to be as bad as he. But moral judgment and emotion are not the same thing. We have been led by the Merchant's narrative, especially by his rhetoric, to make some emotional investment in the relationship, the juxtaposition, of January and May, and I for one find it hard immediately to liquidate the investment. The Merchant, by such devices as first defending May's concern for her honour in his rhetorical outburst against Damian, and then shortly afterwards congratulating her on her womanly resolve to be dishonest—

> Lo, pitee renneth soone in gentil herte!—
> (E1986)

keeps the emotion sloshing back and forth between the weaker and the uglier vessel, frustrating hopes, spoiling values, and maintaining a state of nervousness from which only the most resolutely unflappable reader can free himself.

What seems to me the most triumphant stroke in the Merchant's rhetorical assault on our sensibilities occurs just after May has given Damian a key to the garden of delights and has 'egged' January into asking her to go with him there. The old lecher speaks his invitation:

> 'Ris up, my wif, my love, my lady free;
> The turtles vois is herd, my douve sweete;
> The winter is goon with alle his raines wete.
> Com forth now with thine yën columbin.
> How fairer been thy brestes than is win!
> The garden is enclosed al aboute:
> Com forth, my white spouse! out of doute,
> Thou hast me wounded in myn herte. O wif,
> No spot of thee ne knew I al my lif.
> Com forth and lat us taken oure disport—
> I chees thee for my wif and my confort.'
> Swiche olde lewed wordes used he.
> (E2138-49)

'Such stupid old words he used.' This passage, with its devastating anticlimax, seems to me of itself a sufficient refutation of Bronson's belief 'that there is no intrinsic evidence' that Chaucer wrote the tale 'from a point of view predetermined by such a character' as the Merchant. January's para-phrase of the Song of Solomon comes as close to poetry as the old man ever comes, and at least within hailing distance. Of course the passage has something of his inveterate lust, especially in the final couplet, 'lat us taken oure disport'. But if this were cut off and the rest printed, say, in one of Carleton Brown's collections of Middle English lyrics, I don't think it would shame its company or that any one who did not know would suspect from what context it came. It needs no dedicated patristic critic to point out that in the allegorical tradition the Song of Solomon was taken to represent Christ's love for the Church (or, alternatively, Christ's love for the human soul) and that the love of man and woman, expressed in marriage, was taken to be a mystical analogy of this divine love. Symbolically, the Song of Solomon represented the ideal of marriage. January sullies the symbol in his own way, but the Merchant with his gratuitous sneer wholly destroys its value as an ideal ever to be obtained by human beings. Previously he has dirtied the Creation of Adam and Eve and the rite of marriage, and now he has succeeded in dirtying the theological basis on which marriage was said to rest.

In so doing he has finally allowed the emotional and moral factors of the poem to unite. I dislike moralizing Chaucer's poetry, being persuaded that any work of art that presents an honest picture of existence as seen through any eyes, no matter how jaundiced, hateful, or even wicked the beholder may be, is moral enough of itself. But since I have categorically denied that the Merchant's Tale is primarily a merry jest, I suppose that I am forced to substitute something concrete for the laughter that I refuse to let take over the poem. It seems to me, then, that the Merchant's Tale was most carefully written to present the kind of world that can come into being if a man's approach to love and marriage is wholly mercantile and selfish—if he believes he can buy as a wife a domestic beast that will serve his every wish and, somehow, fulfil his most erotic fantasies. When the beast fails to be in its own right anything more than bestial, the purchaser may, like January, settle for an inner blindness which is more complete than physical blindness; or, like the Merchant, he may deliver himself to hatred—of the disappointing beast, of his own romantic dreams, of marriage, of himself. To read this tale without being disturbed by the force and truth of the Merchant's hatred seems to me impossible.

But I'm still feeling worried about my failure to laugh as loudly as others do. Is my sense of humour not robust enough? Perhaps. I prefer, however, to take refuge in the Merchant's own words in his description of the wedding feast of January and May:

> Whan tendre youthe hath wedded stouping age,
> Ther is swich mirthe that it may nat be writen.
> (E1738-9)

DAVID PARKER

# Can We Trust
## the Wife of Bath?

One of the most lively debates in Chaucer criticism during the past forty years has been between those critics who see Chaucer's characters as individuals, like characters in a modern novel, and those who see them as representative, iconographical figures, devoid of individuality. The iconographical theory seems to command the most respect at present. "The word *characterization*," says D. W. Robertson, Jr., speaking of Chaucer's methods, "is . . . somewhat misleading, since the aim is not to delineate character in a psychological sense but to call attention to abstractions which may manifest themselves in human thought and action." More specifically, he argues, "Alisoun of Bath is not a 'character' in the modern sense at all, but an elaborate iconographic figure designed to show the manifold implications of an attitude."

The scholarship supporting such interpretations was doubtless freed from certain inhibitions by the change in critical climate in the nineteen-twenties, expressed in T. S. Eliot's hostility to "personality" in literature, and in the denunciations of A. C. Bradley's methods in Shakespearean criticism. But most critical revolutions throw up problems as perplexing as the ones their founders sought to solve, if followed too single-mindedly, and this is no exception. There is no problem in admitting that readers have always responded somewhat differently to characters encountered in literature, as distinct from those encountered in their lives, but the iconographical theory, if the distinction it makes is as fundamental as Robertson suggests, entails the belief that characters in fourteenth-century literature cannot in any way be conceived as individuals. We must believe that the fourteenth-century reader

From *The Chaucer Review* 4, no. 2. Copyright © 1969 by The Pennsylvania State University Press.

made an absolute distinction between his experience of the Wife of Bath and his experience of living individuals of his acquaintance. It is difficult to hold to such a belief.

A way of determining how the fourteenth-century reader felt about the relationship between characters in literature and characters in life is to examine the principles of contemporary biography, such as it is, which bridges any gap there might be between the two. It is, of course, normally held that the fourteenth century did not understand the idea of biography as we do, but while it is true that most fourteenth-century "lives" are of aristocrats, kings and saints, figures who are in some way felt to be representative, we can detect, I believe, a feeling in most of them that the truths illustrated are the more striking through being shown as part of the experience of an individual, no matter how exalted. And this feeling, surely, is essential to biography as we understand it. Unless it has some relevance to experience accessible to most human beings biography is incomprehensible.

In the introduction to his poem *The Bruce*, John Barbour speaks of the art of biography in a way most modern biographers would find acceptable. When the poem was composed, in about 1375, Robert the Bruce's death was still a living memory. Barbour announces his intention of telling "a suthfast story":

> For aulde storys that men redys,
> Representis to thaim the dedys
> Of stalwart folk that lywyt ar,
> Rycht as thai than in presence war.

Such verisimilitude is indeed justified morally.

> And, certis, thai suld weill hawe pryss,
> That in ther tyme war wycht and wyss,
> And led thar lyff in gret trawaill,
> And oft in hard stour off bataill
> Wan richt gret price off chewalry,
> And war woydyt off cowardy.
>
> (21-26)

Its value to the reader is homiletic, but a homily works only if the reader believes it to have some relevance to experiences accessible to him. The difference between fourteenth-century and modern biography is that the former displays a much more pronounced and direct interest in the moral consequences and implications of human behavior, but this moral interest is not necessarily divorced from "psychological" interest, and indeed rarely is in a work of any value. Properly speaking, the fourteenth-century biographer, when he was doing his job properly, made no distinction between ethics and psychology.

If the fourteenth-century biographer chose his subjects because they were morally interesting, the fourteenth-century writer of verse-fictions chose or invented his for much the same reasons, and no more than the biographer did he see this moral interest as something that should be detached from human experience. The argument about individual and representative characters in mediaeval literature has in fact got the problem out of focus. The difficulty presented to the modern reader's understanding is not that the fourteenth century saw characters in literature and characters in life differently; rather it is that the fourteenth century understood character differently, wherever it was encountered.

Where the twentieth century is interested in the uniqueness of individuals, the fourteenth was interested in affinities between individuals—which is not quite the same as being uninterested in individuals. Experience accessible to all was demanded, but such experience was acceptable to the reader only if brought home to the sentience of a credible individual. *Everyman*, a later play but in the mediaeval tradition, works not by denying the validity of individual experience, but on the contrary by asserting it. Far from being a moral common denominator, Everyman is an individual, a fact not affected by his standing for every individual at the same time. It is the ability to produce this graceful fusion of the One and the Many, now very rare, that achieves the sense of fatalism, at once passionate and humble, that is one of the peculiar riches of mediaeval literature.

In approaching Chaucer's characters, then, I believe it is profitable at least to reformulate the iconographical theory. The way anyone interprets individual characters, encountered in literature or life, is by comparing his experiences of that character with experiences of character that he has abstracted and conceptualized, with or without the aid of theories. It is surely only rarely that the writer's creation of character doesn't, at least in part, proceed from the same process followed in reverse. There is nearly always some evidence that characters in literature derive in some measure from their author's ideas about what makes and moulds character in general. It is usually possible to explain the behavior of fictional characters by reference to ideas about character good for more than the particular individual in question.

It is strange, therefore, that the fact it is possible to explain Chaucer's characters has been taken as proving that none are intended as individuals. I find it requires a peculiar effort of the imagination, which a wider reading of fourteenth-century literature fails to justify, to believe that Chaucer's specification of name, sex, station, appearance, history, disposition and so on was intended only as the elaboration of an icon that the reader was supposed to dissociate from his own experience of people. Chaucer was interested in character traits that, as scholarship has shown us, could be classified and explained, but no more so than many twentieth-century novelists, and no one supposes that their characters are not so much intended as individuals as, say, elaborate Freudian types.

The pilgrims of the *Canterbury Tales*, it is my contention, are all, to a varying degree, to be taken as individuals. Some are certainly less individualized: the Knight, the Parson, and the Plowman, for instance; but it would be a mistake, I feel, to say they are idealized, without qualifying this as something not irreconcilable with a species of realism. Each in his own way emulates a moral ideal that demands the suppression of individuality, and we ought to give Chaucer and his age the benefit of the doubt by allowing that some people managed to live up to ideals. The artifice comes not in characterization, but in the way Chaucer creates a pattern among his pilgrims of contrasts and correspondencies.

That Chaucer possessed at least a poetic apprehension of individual personality is evident, I think, in his irony. For irony to be effective, it is necessary that the reader see the figure against whom it is directed as an individual, if only fleetingly, in order that the incipient craving for vengeance in our desire for justice be gratified. You can't be revenged on an abstraction.

Chaucer's ironies against his pilgrims are usually more complex and more delicate than those corresponding to this sketch of the crudest sort, just as his characters are more complex and delicate than those afforded by the crudest methods of characterization. Consider a passage from Chaucer's description of the Prioress in the *General Prologue*:

> But, for to speken of hire conscience,
> She was so charitable and so pitous
> She wolde wepe, if that she saugh a mous
> Kaught in a trappe, if it were deed or bledde.
> Of smale houndes hadde she that she fedde
> With rosted flessh, or milk and wastel-breed.
> But soore wepte she if oon of hem were deed,
> Or if men smoot it with a yerde smerte;
> And al was conscience and tendre herte.
> (A 142-50)

The ambivalence of judgment in this passage has been pointed out many times. The delicate balance and generosity of the irony has been less remarked on. Rather than being made simply indignant with the Prioress, the reader is required to respond to both judgments suggested: that love of animals is a misdirection of Christian charity, and that, with or without other virtues, love of animals is good. The reader is compelled by the irony to respond to the Prioress as an individual, to see her complexity, and to exercise the complex sort of judgment human beings exact.

Among all the characters of the *Canterbury Tales*, it is the Wife of Bath whose individuality is least easily explained away. There is a sense of abundant life about her, not least evident in the contradictions in her speech and behavior. Walter Clyde Curry's splendid analysis of the astrological influences governing her contradictory nature may be interpreted in two ways. We may see it either as evidence that Chaucer was interested only in the moral and psychological types resulting from particular astrological conjunctions, or as evidence that he was interested in explaining the character and behavior of individuals. Curry himself admits an inclination to favor the latter view. "Under the spell of Chaucer's pen," he says, "one rests under the illusion that the Wife of Bath is a complex human being."

Another contradiction, that between the Wife's theory and her practice, has been demonstrated by Charles A. Owen, Jr. Her professed beliefs in female sovereignty in marriage, he points out, are not finally followed by the heroine of her tale, who obeys her husband: "And she obeyed hym in every thyng / That myghte doon hym plesance or likyng" (D 1255-56). And her own claim to having exercised "maistrie" over her fifth husband is to be doubted after these words:

> After that day we hadden never debaat.
> God helpe me so, I was to hym as kynde
> As any wyf from Denmark unto Ynde,
> And also trewe, and so was he to me.
> (822-25)

If Curry's interpretation of the Wife's character is conformable to seeing her as no individual, Owen's suggests a personality complicated to a degree at which it becomes absurd to deny individuality. I should like to examine a further contradiction in her speech that suggests further - complexities of character, and through which, it even appears, Chaucer allows the reader a dramatic glimpse into her inner life.

My chief contention is that the Wife of Bath is not fully to be trusted, and my evidence for this is to be found in the contradictions between two passages in the *Wife of Bath's Prologue.* In one of these, ending with the lines quoted by Owen, she offers, as proof of her theory of "maistrie," an account of the resolution of the quarrel between her fifth husband and herself:

> But atte laste, with muchel care and wo,
> We fille acorded by us selven two.
> He yaf me al the bridel in myn hond,
> To han the governance of hous and lond,
> And of his tonge, and of his hond also;
> And made hym brenne his book anon right tho.
> And whan that I hadde geten unto me,
> By maistrie, al the soveraynetee,
> And that he seyde, "Myn owene trewe wyf,
> Do as thee lust the terme of al thy lyf;

Keep thyn honour, and keep eek myn estaat"—
After that day we hadden never debaat.
God helpe me so, I was to hym as kynde
As any wyf from Denmark unto Ynde,
And also trewe, and so was he to me.

(811-25)

But another passage, three hundred lines earlier, tells a different story.

Now of my fifthe housbonde wol I telle.
God lete his soule nevere come in helle!
And yet was he to me the mooste shrewe;
That feele I on my ribbes al by rewe,
And evere shal unto myn endyng day.
But in oure bed he was so fressh and gay,
And therwithal so wel koude he me glose,
Whan that he wolde han my *bele chose*,
That thogh he hadde me bete on every bon,
He koude wynne agayn my love anon.
I trowe I loved hym best, for that he
Was of his love daungerous to me.
We wommen han, if that I shal nat lye,
In this matere a queynte fantasye;
Wayte what thyng we may nat lightly have,
Therafter wol we crie al day and crave.
Forbede us thyng, and that desiren we;
Preesse on us faste, and thanne wol we fle.
With daunger oute we al oure chaffare;
Greet prees at market maketh deere ware,
And to greet cheep is holde at litel prys:
This knoweth every womman that is wys.

(503-24)

It is difficult to square these two statements. The usual way of understanding the earlier passage is to assume that the Wife is talking about the
time before she had subdued Jankyn. If this is so it is odd that her most
evidently cherished recollections of the marriage should be of the period that,
by her own account, was the least delightful.

The first passage I quoted (the later in the text) is a carefully calculated conclusion to an anecdote the Wife tells, with the intention of illustrat-
ing the truth of her theory of marriage. It is dominated by her wish to prove
her point, that a husband need only to submit to the will of his wife for marital
happiness to be ensured. This is what happened in her fifth marriage, she says.

The way in which the Wife seems to be trying to get the best of both
worlds, in this passage, suggesting that she was both in command and
obedient, as Owen has pointed out, disturbs our belief in its veracity. The
earlier passage does so even more, suggesting that the happiest part of their

marriage was not a period of peace following a quarrel, with the Wife strictly in command. Unlike the later passage, it is a spontaneous aside, following automatically on the Wife's thinking of her fifth husband, and occurring before she has begun to fit him into her pet theory. What she spontaneously remembers is not how she commanded Jankyn, but how he would beat her and then win her round by love-making.

This passage in fact suggests that the passage about her assumption of "maistrie" is either untrue, or a considerable distortion of the facts. We can assume either that she didn't win the sovereignty she claims to have done, or that she did, and found it less agreeable than she had hoped.

From what she says of her other marriages and from her digression on "daunger," we may be sure that she would have had little but contempt for a submissive Jankyn. The theory of "daunger" as she expresses it, partly no doubt to scandalize the forces of masculine convention she is addressing, but also, there is no reason to doubt, in all sincerity, is in radical conflict with her theory of "maistrie." "Daunger" is both a technique used by women—"With daunger oute we al oure chaffare"—and a perversity of feeling from which they suffer, and through which they may be exploited:

> Wayte what thyng we may nat lightly have,
> Therafter wol we crie al day and crave.
> Forbede us thyng, and that desiren we;
> Preesse on us faste, and thanne wol we fle.

The digression follows an explicit statement that she loved Jankyn best because he exploited this perversity of feeling: "I trowe I loved hym best, for that he / Was of his love daungerous to me." Those whose sympathy Chaucer's art enlists on the Wife of Bath's side will hope, both for her sake and Jankyn's, that her claim finally to have achieved "maistrie" is untrue. To have been happy she would have needed, according to her own analysis of the nature of women, to be continually frustrated in her striving for "maistrie." Its achievement would have been disappointing; "to greet cheep is holde at litel prys."

There is sufficient evidence in the contrasting tones of the two passages that she was so luckily frustrated. The smug formality of the summing-up of her argument excites not nearly so much confidence in its veracity as the energy of her more spontaneous reflections:

> But atte laste, with muchel care and wo,
> We fille acorded by us selven two. . . .

Contrast this with,

> Now of my fifthe housbonde wol I telle.
> God lete his soule nevere come in helle. . . .

If we accept the Wife of Bath as a character, I believe we are forced to admit that she is a character whose word is not to be trusted. Chaucer shows her as a woman who delights in fantasies about her own life, partly because they please her and partly because she enjoys shocking others with them, but which are exploded by her own accidental self-revelations in the contradictions between statements she makes about her past. In the tensions between the fantasies and the reality we get a glimpse of her inner life.

Not to accept the Wife of Bath as a character creates some peculiar problems. There is first of all the problem, already discussed in general terms, of believing that the fourteenth-century reader could erect an impenetrable barrier between his interpretations of literary and of living human beings. The belief that he did not do this is of course not susceptible to proof, but the sheer oddity of believing otherwise, of believing that he ignored the invitation in the text, so palpable to twentieth-century readers, to participate in the act of creation and construct a human identity for the Wife, is so great that it is surprising so few have hitherto noticed it.

The other problem is explaining the Wife's inconsistencies, other than by putting them down to Chaucer's bungling. The least we can ask of an iconographical figure is that it be consistent in its symbolic austerity. If the Wife is simply iconographical, then we must treat her rather like those early mediaeval paintings in which the bodies of figures point one way and their feet another; she must be seen as a quaint illustration of the limitations of mediaeval art. Most readers, I think, for whom everything the Wife of Bath does and says is "in character," would hesitate before choosing such a brutal interpretation, rather than reconciling the inconsistencies in a complex character.

In depicting the Wife of Bath as an individual, I have argued, Chaucer was only doing what other fourteenth-century poets tried to do. What is unusual is the way she, like a number of Chaucer's characters, survives as a recognizable individual into the twentieth century. The difficulty of recognition over the centuries is minimized. Whether Chaucer's sensibility anticipated the shift in human consciousness we describe as the renaissance, or whether he was simply profoundly aware of human beings, he achieved this feat by creating a character not in harmony but in conflict with itself. Many of the ingredients of the Wife's personality may be unfamiliar to the modern reader, but the way they are mixed he recognizes instantly. It is a measure of Chaucer's greatness that he is thus able to penetrate the ephemeral details of human life to conditions that are timeless.

ALICE S. MISKIMIN

# From Medieval to Renaissance:
# Some Problems in Historical Criticism

*History . . . cannot say, and indeed hardly ever knows, what it is omitting,
nor can it ever know how this comes about.*

—PAUL VALERY

S tudy of the influence of a masterpiece
in any art reveals that from the very first, in the accumulating frames of its
early reputation and imitation, its fame becomes a part of the artifact itself.
As for poetry, as Wellek put it, "Every reading of a poem is more than the
genuine poem." It is virtually impossible now to read the Great Books—the
*Odyssey,* the *Aeneid,* the *Commedia*—without knowing that they are Great
Books; they have been read for us.

"So it is, that here as elsewhere, what men seek for, that generally do
they find. . . ." Thus Caroline Spurgeon somewhat wearily concluded the
introduction to her monumental history of Chaucer's fame, *Five Hundred
Years of Chaucer Criticism and Allusion, 1357–1900.* Ideally, criticism should
attempt to refer a work of art, or a poem, both to the values of its own time
and to all periods subsequent to its own, for "a work of art is both 'eternal' (it
preserves a certain identity), and 'historical' (it passes through a process of
traceable development)." Such a historical critique of Chaucer is worthy of
aspiration, but it has yet to be achieved. Modern medievalists are still
embroiled in questions of methodology, following the precedents set for the
classics. Confronted with a judgment with which he cannot agree, Peter
Dronke asks, "Is not *this* the anachronism, reading into the text what the

writer has not intended, in order to comply with modern notions of the medieval?" From the other side of the historians' circle, perhaps we hear Curtius's reply: "It is immaterial whether the catalogue of ships is [interpolated] by a Homerid or not: we should read Homer as he was read for two thousand years." For Chaucer, five hundred years have certainly not been long enough.

Almost three-quarters of another century have been added to Spurgeon's *Five Hundred Years*; the "Chaucerians" have been disposed of, sooner and more easily than the Homerids. The manuscripts, all posthumous, are being reedited, for the second time in this century, and the *Chaucer Life Records*, edited by M. M. Crow and Clair Olson, finally published in 1966, seem to have established the biographical facts for the first time since the fifteenth century. Hammond's *Bibliographical Manual* of 1908 has been brought up to date by D. D. Griffith's volume for 1908–53 and William Crawford's for 1954–63; student guides to the literature, such as that of Albert Baugh, provide virtually annual supplements. It has become clear that Chaucer the poet is no longer in danger of being buried under the weight of his reputation, but he is still imprisoned in it. The purpose of this book is to look back to the beginnings of his poetic influence, to the earlier periods of Chaucer's fame, when the medieval Chaucer gradually evolved into the forefather figure of Renaissance English literary history.

As with Homer, so with "English Homer," as Chaucer was named by Renaissance historians. It is unlikely that a modern critic can find a single line left in the canon that has not been glossed, a date or occasion yet to propose. But of course the work still flourishes, and old certainties are open to challenge. The only presumably fixed date in the chronology of Chaucer's poems, that of the elegy for Blanche of Lancaster, *The Book of the Duchess*, has recently been questioned, and the vexed issue of final-*e*—Chaucer's rhythms—submitted to a new scrutiny. In any review of the conflicting testimony to the vigor of medieval poetry, in the past half-century's yield of brilliant scholarly and critical readings of Chaucer and his contemporaries, it soon becomes clear that new orthodoxies and true believers, as convinced as those of the nominalist and realist parties of late medieval theology, still are at odds in the field, occupying positions as diametrically opposed as the schoolmen. "If Chaucer means what Professor X says he does, he cannot possibly be saying what Professor Y explains he means." Provided with facing pages of gloss, interlinear translations, prose paraphrase, and heavy annotation, readers are reminded of their own ignorance and become humbly confused, diverted from the poems to the marginalia, the spectacular display of critical scholarship that would seem to illuminate every detail. All too often contentious, however, and incongruous to Chaucer's wit and humility, the debates of modern expositors are in effect un-Chaucerian in tone and conviction, but to readers of Spurgeon's anthology, classically familiar.

In criticism as in logic, it should be never forgotten that *negativa non sunt probanda*: absence of particular meanings can never be proved. An interpretation can be said to be corroborated only if we are unable to find refuting evidence, rather than if we are able to find supporting evidence; it is a historical commonplace that "of nearly every theory it may be said that it agrees with many facts," which are a dime-a-dozen, empirically, and easily chosen a priori to confirm hypotheses. Circular reasoning and the selection of evidence in the light of the very theory the evidence is supposed to test flourish in all our criticism and are rooted deep in the past. In the readings of the medieval and Renaissance Chaucer which follow, I shall question and try to test some of the assumptions of contemporary criticism as to the varieties of meaning in allegory and the uses of analogy, against historical evidence. The metamorphosis of one poet's book, from manuscript to print, provides a paradigm of literary evolution. As a case history, we can inquire how the medieval Chaucer's book became an antiquity within two hundred years by processes of which contemporaries were becoming acutely aware.

This study, based on facts long known and commonplace formulae, is presented, then, not as a new approach or prologue to Chaucer, but as a supplement or epilogue, an ex post facto inquiry into early "readings" of Chaucer which in striking ways both resemble and parody his own readings of his *auctors*. The familiar tag, *as the book seyth*, however, implies questions of poetic originality and elements of imitation which in late medieval and early Renaissance poems are concealed, controversial, and perhaps insolubly conjectural. The disappearance of such phrases in the early sixteenth century is itself revealing and raises the question of what takes their place. As has long been known, the first translation of a Petrarchan sonnet into English—more than a century before Wyatt—is Chaucer's borrowed, and unacknowledged, version of "S'amor non e," which Troilus sings in *Troilus and Criseyde*. Chaucer has altered the Italian in significant details which affect interpretation, but, given the variables, what conclusions can be drawn? Was it a bad manuscript, or scribal error, or inadequate knowledge of Italian, or conscious revision, intended for characterization of the speaker? How can ironies be certified? The questions of Chaucerian irony, latent in the text, unlike those of his "sources," remain open for speculation, for they underlie the "medieval" reading of the poems, and their rereading in the Renaissance.

Given the richness and variety of the historical evidence we have inherited, it is possible to reexamine and reassess the literary implications of *myn auctor* and the *olde bokes* in Chaucer's poems, and observe their afterlife in literary history, as topoi—means by which *auctoritee* and postmedieval poetic influence descend during the two-hundred-year evolution of the English humanists. Within five years of Petrarch's coronation in Rome as poet laureate, Richard de Bury, the former tutor of Edward III and later bishop of Durham and lord chancellor of England, described the peregrinations of the

Muses to the North—the arrival of the first seeds of the Renaissance, in his *Philobiblon* (1345). The *translatio studii* topos is proudly applied to England:

> The admirable Minerva seems to have made the tour of the nations of mankind, and casually come in contact with them all, from one end of the world to the other, that she might communicate herself to each. We perceive her to have passed through the Indians, Babylonians, Egyptians, Greeks, Arabians, and Latins. She next deserted Athenas, and then retired from Rome; and having already given the slip to the Parisians, she has at last happily reached Britain, that most renowned of islands... the Microcosm.

One of the most learned men in England, de Bury was one of the first to read Greek, and he quotes, with approval, Plato's *Phaedo*. The library he founded at Durham College, Oxford, was scattered when the college was dissolved by Henry VIII, but his passionate little treatise in defense of learning and vindication of poetry was printed in 1473; it prophesies Sidney's *Apology*. The literary history of the English Renaissance began in the fourteenth century, as the Renaissance historians themselves saw.

But after 1400, Chaucer's late fourteenth-century world became immediately, then ever more distantly, a shadowed past. The deposition of Richard II, virtually coincident with Chaucer's death, was to contemporaries truly an end, and the Lancastrian accession a new order. The new century began with a turbulent sense of transition and sharp memories of the ending century's turmoil, in both politics and religion. Paradoxically, it is often the case that the immediate successors of those familiar with a historical episode are the ones who have the greatest difficulty remembering what it was really like. The blur of change—in language as in the image of events—occurs in a single generation. Imagination, memory, and the invoking of authorities begin to conflict. Then revision is under way. Vico found his historical theory, the *universali fantastici*, in this very conflict: those universal ideas return, originating in fantasy, by means of which the imagination seeks to ward off chaos. He saw them as formulae which become institutionalized, stereotyped—as magic, ritual, social orders—ultimately reducible to rhetoric. For Vico, anticipating Freud, poetry is an autonomous mode of perception, of self-orientation, a defense against the flux. For poets within the flux, from Chaucer to Spenser and Shakespeare, the issue of time's disintegration is not so simply stated. Mutability, as a reflex of the invocation of authority, becomes a constant theme in evocations of the medieval past. The mutability of language, and of the meaning of poetry itself, confront every reader of Chaucer's book.

The Middle Ages slowly became "medieval" as the paradox of receding time seemed gradually to reveal the periodization of events, of ideas, of culture itself—as in de Bury's welcome to the Muses. The German Protestant annalist Cellarius appears to have been one of the first to use *medii aevi* in its present sense, in the seventeenth century. He saw the period as extending from the fall of Constantine to the fall of Constantinople, from 340 to 1453 A.D. As Curtius drily comments, "Middle Ages is (as a concept) . . . scientifically preposterous, but indispensable for mutual comprehension; whether one is to distinguish 'renaissances' is a question of expedience." The present, still indefinite, meaning of Middle Age, the period between "ancient" and "modern" times, seems to have become common shortly after 1700, competing with "Gothic." The earliest citation in the Oxford English Dictionary, for 1722, indicates prevalent common usage of the term. *Medieval* (translating the scholarly *medium aevum*) is quoted from the *Gentleman's Magazine* in 1827, twenty-five years before Ruskin's lectures refined and popularized it. Nevertheless, it would seem that soon after 1400, men were already conscious of the end of an era, and looked back to it, ambivalently, as inheritors. In the historical framework of this book, the relationships between medieval Chaucer and his *auctors*, and those of his Renaissance successors who then looked back to him as their progenitor, are separated as two contingent problems. The time span is roughly two hundred years, from the reading of Chaucer's poems by his audience of contemporaries to the readings of Elizabethans, as witnessed in Shakespeare and Spenser. It goes without saying that modern interpretation of the Renaissance Chaucer is probably no less biased and arbitrary than theirs was of their medieval forebears. Our chief advantage is the purity of our texts.

Chaucer's Renaissance reputation and his poetic influence, as himself an *auctor*, among literary historians and poets, are distinct phenomena which are in turn distinct from a third, the poems on which the fame and *auctoritee* depend: manuscripts, printed texts, editions. The original manuscripts have long been gone, but early copies and the Renaissance editions remain to be read for what they can tell us of their readers. Among readers in the Middle Ages and in the Renaissance we need to distinguish between poets, who read one another with special privileges, critics, whose interpretations may be disinterested or not, and finally, the silent audience addressed within the poem: *thou, redere*, the hypothetical ideal solitary for whom poems are written. The last is the most important of all and, for the reading of Chaucer, indispensable. Anticipating the structuralists, T. S. Eliot in 1919 restated more elegantly what scholiasts and pedants from the Alexandrian librarians to Isidore of Seville had always assumed: poetry exists in horizontal time, in the synchronous limbo of the *olde bokes*. There, medieval poems live with all poems, their literary ancestors, contemporaries, and successors. We read Chaucer as we read his Virgil, Ovid, Boethius, and Dante, as did Shakespeare, Dryden, Spenser, and Keats. In Eliot's sense, we might disregard the medieval and Renaissance audience, *ars poetica, movere et docere*, as irrelevant to us. Thus we may immediately avoid the infinite regress of revisionary history in which every age redefines and reinvents its past. To do so seems to escape the traps—the questions of Langland's audience and Chaucer's contemporaries, the early marginalia and annotations in the manuscripts, the accretions of Chauceriana in the new editions of the poems after 1500—the only evidence that survives to witness medieval and early Renaissance readings of the poems. The difficulties and risks of error in historical interpretation are admittedly real and not irrelevant, but excessive caution is as misleading as excessive boldness, and a half-truth is a half-truth in any period. For both the medieval Chaucer and the Renaissance Chaucer, the contemporary world has to be taken into account as an imperfect historical given, by inference and implication, insofar as the limitations of our knowledge and subjectivity permit. Few have entered the labyrinth of literary history between 1400 and 1600, and fewer still have emerged able to say what they saw. The phenomenon of metamorphosis takes place, but no one has yet fully understood and described how. C. S. Lewis has surely gone further than any other modern reader, and all who come after pay him homage. I have found, however, that his account of the Renaissance Chaucer raises almost as many questions as those he answered, and instead of certainty, left much in doubt. My debt to him, and to other great modern Chaucerians, will be apparent in these studies, as will my divergence from prevailing views.

## ANONYMITY AND ACKNOWLEDGMENT: THE MEDIEVAL AUTHOR, *AUCTORITEE*, AND TIME

It has often been suggested that Chaucer momentarily drops his mask as narrator and becomes himself, in replying to the nameless Friend who stops him on the way out of his House of Fame:

> Frend, what is thy name?
> Artow come hider to han fame?
> Nay, for sothe, frend, quod y;
> I cam noght hyder, graunt mercy,
> For no such cause, by my hed!
> Sufficeth me, as I were ded,
> That no wight have my name in honde.
> I wot myself best how y stonde;
> For what I drye, or what I thynke,
> I wil myselven al hyt drynke,
> Certeyn, for the more part,
> As fer forth as I kan myn art.

But Chaucer has of course already begged the question, having named his narrator "Geffrey" in the self-ridiculing comedy of the second part of the poem. Chaucer's thirst for fame is a curious corollary issue in this poem, and it is worth comparing it to Petrarch's imagined confession of his egotism to "Augustine" in the *Secretum*. In this dialogue, Petrarch tries to defend his insatiable desire for earthly glory as the first natural step toward "that which awaits us in heaven." More Boethian than the *Trionfi*, the *Secretum* expresses the anxiety of the Christian humanist poet confronting his ignorance and mortality and the ambiguity of Fame. Petrarch imagines Augustine's rebuke:

> Augustine: You trust to your intellectual powers and your reading of many books; you glory in the beauty of your language and take delight in the comeliness of your mortal frame. But do you now perceive in how many respects your skill does not equal that of the obscurest of mankind, not to speak of weak and lowly animals, whose works no effort on your part could possibly imitate? Exult then if you can in your abilities! And your reading, what does it profit you? From the mass that you have read, how much sticks in your mind, how much takes root and brings forth fruit in its season? Examine your mind and you will find that all you know, if compared with your own ignorance, would bear to it the same relation as that borne to the ocean by a tiny brook, shrunk by the summer heats.

Both Petrarch and Chaucer (unlike Gower in his *Confessio*) defied their imagined confessors; the unfinished *Trionfi* and the broken-off *Book of Fame* were set aside, but not to spurn poetry, and both finished other poems more immediately apprehensible. Difference, however, tells more than likeness: Petrarch's fear that Laura's name might be misconstrued forever with his own laurel, his anxiety that men might think he envied Dante, could never disturb his English reader Chaucer, who hardly presumed so much, never named a Lady of his own (although he suffered for Criseyde and for Alison of Bath), and borrowed Dante's golden eagle to satirize his own narrator's unsurpassed *lewedness*. Perhaps he did not invent the Temple or the *Book* "to han fame," but Chaucer did leave his name, as Bennett points out, for the first time in an English poem in which the narrator names himself. He set a precedent and left the enigmatic identity of "Geffrey the poet" as a conundrum for criticism. In spite of the modest disclaimer, "Sufficeth me, as I were ded That no wight have my name in honde," Chaucer knew how he stood, and he went on, "as fer forth as I kan myn art."

The *Book of Fame* explores the limits of poetic ambiguity, and Bennett is surely right to emphasize Chaucer's ambivalence everywhere in it, as he hovers "between two worlds, celestial and terrestrial . . . between jest and earnest, faith in dreams and scepticism." Perhaps he is also right that the chief difference between Boethian resignation to the mutability of time's curse on poets, "the whiche writynges long and dirk eelde / doth awey, bothe hem and ek hir auctours" (*Boece*, 2.7.88–90), and the attitude of Petrarch and Chaucer lies in Boethius's despair of the "trustworthiness of writers and the permanence of their works," which Renaissance poetics affirm, and medieval poetics doubt. The questions raised in the *Book of Fame*, and therein left unanswered, epitomize Chaucer's allegorical irony, "that which affirms and denies at the same time," as I shall subsequently attempt to describe it.

As everyone knows, Chaucer invented very little of his own; like Shakespeare, he found what he needed at hand. The brilliant source studies of modern scholars—Bennett, Bloomfield, Payne, Pratt, Muscatine—have revealed the dovetailing procedures under the surface of Chaucer's synthetic dream visions, as well as in *Troilus* and the *Canterbury Tales*. The Temples of Venus and Fame are variously modeled on Claudian, Guido de Columnis, and the Temple of Juno in the *Aeneid*. The earthly paradises variously come from Jean de Meung, Dante, and Alan de Lille; the lists of trees from Guillaume de Lorris and Statius, and the catalogue of trees burned at Arcita's funeral in Boccaccio's *Teseide*. Translated elements are always fused by the devices of the Chaucerian dreamer, but, named and unnamed, the *auctoritees* lie under the patterns of allusion and figurative imagery like a mosaic floor seen through water. It is still difficult to tell whose dreams these are, but to the reader of the Renaissance Chaucer, as we shall see, it was virtually impossible to distinguish Chaucer's from these of his imitators. The dream visions are, we now know, more authentic than the "Chaucers Dreme" Speght unveiled in his folio of 1598, but authentic in a highly sophisticated sense. The modern recovery of so many of Chaucer's *auctoritees* in effect heightens the sense of the dubious meanings of *auctor* associated with Rumor, Alison, the Pardoner, and Pandarus—masters of quotation—and intensifies the incongruity between the naive Dreamer and his very subtle dreams. It is more apparent to us than it could have been to the Elizabethan reader that the autonomy of the poet as a "maker" of fictions was already a problem, concealed in the circumlocutions of medieval poetics, and that new meanings of the word "invention" were coming to the surface, soon made explicit in Henryson's most Chaucerian poem. No less self-conscious than Petrarch in feigning simplicity, Chaucer was as aware as the Italians he admired of the unpredictable secret arts of writing, not merely for a present audience but for unseen readers and for the future. The "new" poet is not just a compiler of stories or transmitter of authorities, but the originator of a complex, silent, and irreversible creative process. Acute awareness is also the indispensable element in Chaucer's irony—his detachment—and, for whatever other virtues they may share, Petrarch's fame was not for wit, the special wittiness that transcends the comic and becomes philosophical. Chaucer's irony is closer to Boethius's, in his cross-examination of Philosophy, than to Petrarch's in his homage to Fame; he is always nearer to self-doubt than to pride. But the medieval Chaucer has more in common with the irony of Socrates, it seems to me, than with any of his contemporaries or successors. The Renaissance Plato and the Renaissance Chaucer were venerated for myths that confirmed the sixteenth-century image; hence Chaucer's scepticism, and Plato's attacks on poetry, had to be explained away, rationalized, or forgotten. So Chaucer was taken for a Wycliffite and a precursor of the Reformation; his more profound doubts as to the efficacy of any *auctoritees* at all were no longer apparent.

Beginning with Caxton, who in the 1480's first supplied an "ending" for the unfinished *Book of Fame*, through the early sixteenth-century editions of Pynson, Thynne, and their successors later in the century, the emergent Tudor revisions of the historical, public aspects of Chaucer's world were revising at the same time the conceptions of "medieval" art, always excepting Chaucer and Gower from censure. The interdiction of the old Catholic hegemony was finally proclaimed in England by statute and made official in the Act of 1542, "For the Advancement of true Religion and thabolissment of the contrarie. . . ." The act provides for utter abolishment of forbidden books, but "Chaucers bokes, Caunterburye Tales, and Gowers books [are exempt] and shall not be comprehended in the prohibicions of this acte." The intervening historical events, before and after 1542-43, permitted and indeed stimulated increasing self-consciousness among later Tudor humanists and earlier Elizabethan poets and their audiences, who now looked back to Chaucer's and Gower's proscribed medieval world through the Renaissance new vision of society, a world to be enriched by the making of new art. One honors one's ancestors, but were they indeed greater or lesser than ourselves? Who can see more? Lucan's aphorism, "We are but pygmies, standing on the shoulders of giants" (*nani gigantum humeris insidentes* in Bernard of Chartres), is the theme of homage in Petrarch's letters to Cicero and Homer. It is heard again and again, and interpreted both ways: to repudiate, and to revere, the past.

The proud Elizabethan sense of advance beyond the predecessors is stated clearly in Puttenham's praise of Wyatt and Surrey in 1589, as the first reformers of English meter and style,

> hauing trauailed into Italie, and there tasted the sweete and stately measures and stile of the Italian Poesie as nouices newly crept out of the schooles of Dante Arioste and Petrarch, they greatly pollished our rude and homely maner of vulgar Poesie, from that it had bene before.

Webbe speaks with similar contempt of the "brutish poetry of rhyme" in 1586, exempting Chaucer, and oddly, Langland, for his anticipation of the blank verse line. But it is not until Francis Bacon, after 1600, that the new conception of time's maturing is stated with full confidence and without equivocation: "The old times are in reality the youth of the world, and the present is therefore more mature and wiser." Bacon's fuller statement of the theme comes in the *Novum Organum* of 1620, in the eighty-fourth aphorism of the first book:

Men have been kept back as by a kind of enchantment by reverence for antiquity, by the authority of men accounted great in philosophy, and then by general consent. As for antiquity, . . . the old age of the world is to be accounted the true antiquity, and this is the attribute of our own time, not that in which the ancients lived . . . which, though in respect of us it was the elder, yet in respect of the world it was the younger. . . . Surely it would be disgraceful if, while the regions of the material globe of the earth, of the sea, and of the stars, have been in our time laid widely opened and revealed, and the intellectual globe should remain shut up within the narrow limits of the old discoveries. . . .

And with regard to authority, it shows a feeble mind to grant so much to authors, and yet to deny time his rights, who is the author of authors, nay, rather of all authority. For rightly is truth called the daughter of time, not of authority. It is no wonder if those enchantments of antiquity and authority and consent have so bound up men's powers that they have been made impotent, like persons bewitched, to accompany with the nature of things.

Carlo Cipolla, commenting on the coincidence of the emergence of printed books, the Reformation, and the Counter-Reformation, noted that as more men learned to read, supply was stimulated to keep pace with demand: books become increasingly cheaper and their use more widespread. But both the growth of pedagogy and the rise of vernacular literatures in Europe are "the unfortunate byproducts of the religious feud . . . of book-burning, bigotry, control over schools, and censorship of publication." Printing, after 1500, speeded up the growth of literacy and spread of reading, and it also heightened scholarly consciousness of linguistic evolution. In England, new editions of old books aroused interest in Anglo-Saxon studies and called attention to the primitive state of medieval literature; antiquarian research began to bring back to life archaisms frozen in the texts of Caxton, Pynson, and William Thynne. Francis Thynne, in his *Animadversions* on Speght (1599), speaks for the first time in English since Caxton as a textual critic of Chaucer's language:

so that, of necessyte, both in matter, myter, and meaning, yt must needs gather corruptione, passyng through so manye handes, as the water dothe, the further it runneth from the pure founteyne.

Thynne is well aware of his "source"—Spenser's Chaucerian "pure well of English undefil'd"—and he is using the water imagery ironically. Speght's 1598 edition of Chaucer's *Works* is the first to contain a separate glossary of obsolete and difficult words, consciously anticipating the reader's needs; the list is nearly doubled in size in Speght's "revised" edition of 1602. Writing in the same year, Samuel Daniel concluded his *Defence of Rime* with a troubled awareness of uncertain judgment, not of the present, but of the future— without Bacon's optimism—as it seemed to a poet defending both the *olde bookes* and his own. His *Defence* of native English style is on historical grounds, in answer to Campion's humanist contempt for the barbarous vernacular:

> [Literary standards are] things that are continually in a wandring motion, carried with the violence of our uncertaine likings, being but onely the time that gives them their power. . . . [This inordinate desire of innovation] is but a Character of that perpetuall revolution which wee see to be in all things that never remaine the same, and we must heerein be content to submit ourselves to the law of time, which in a few yeeres will make al that, for which we now contend, Nothing.

But what is more significant is what is omitted in Daniel's *Defence* of the English past. In reply to the charge that "all lay pittifully deformed in those lacke-learning times, from the declining of the Romane Empire, till the light of the Latine tongue was revived [by the Renaissance humanists Erasmus, Reuchlin, and More]" Daniel chooses to cite the eloquence and learning of the Venerable Bede, Joseph of Exeter, Roger Bacon, and Occam, but not one English poet of the later Middle Ages. He does not name Chaucer or Gower in his list of precedents for the poetry of his own time, but he eulogizes instead Petrarch and Boccaccio, whose excellence in Italian surpassed anything written "in any other form." It was Italy, "the miracle and phoenix of the world, which wakened up other Nations likewise with this desire of glory," long before time brought forth Reuchlin, Erasmus, and More. Of Chaucer's "ancient" English rhyme, Daniel has nothing to say.

Although it is taken for granted that we know what "medieval" and "Renaissance" mean, it is very difficult to persuade historians to define them. In effect, since Ruskin's popular triumphs finally established the French term *renaissance* in English in the 1850's the old idea, once clear in Italy, has become an elastic historical illusion. In literary history, "Renaissance" encompasses the diverse succession of period styles from Chaucer's descendants Skelton, Wyatt, Surrey, and Spenser ("Tudor," "Humanist," "Elizabethan") through the early years of Milton's poetic apprenticeship ("Metaphysical," "Jacobean," "Caroline," "Baroque"). Our anachronisms and overlapping terms are the obvious result of nineteenth-century pattern making, as interesting phenomena in themselves as Vico's spirals. The term "Renaissance" was, however, in origin continental, and it seems, in English, to obscure rather than to make things clear. Cultural phenomena occurring in the north of Europe after ca. 1500 are seemingly made analogous to the Italian humanists' enunciation of recovery of the ancient world, which began before Chaucer was born. English literary theory in the sixteenth century rests in part on the premises of Italian poets and critics of the fourteenth. Thus Boccaccio and Petrarch, first translated by Chaucer before 1400, returned to England in the second, greater wave of Italian translations from 1550-1600.

But Italian as a foreign language did not seem to have so profoundly changed, as the Middle English of Chaucer had become decayed: to Elizabethans, fourteenth-century English poetry looked far more "antique" than fourteenth-century Italian.

Of course, both "medieval" and "Renaissance" are opinions, anachronistic, and no more than convenient abstractions, to be redefined each time a new historian announces he has found proof they ever—or never—existed, in the twelfth, fourteenth, or sixteenth century. As classifications for art and ideas, they are at once usefully vague and irritatingly specific. They frequently obfuscate the mind, rather than free it to see more in the light of general meaning. It is paradoxical to alternate comparisons by epithets of this kind, "medieval Chaucer," "Renaissance Chaucer," for they coexist in the same body, the same mind, the same poems. As Donaldson remarks of the Wife of Bath, "if [her] Prologue were the only literature to survive between 1200 and 1600, one might say that in her character the Renaissance sprang from the Middle Ages." Reading the same Chaucerian text, Auerbach comments:

> There is hardly a sign of humanism. Chaucer still makes a considerable display of semi-erudite exempla, taken over from the earlier Middle Ages; the effect is often rather grotesque, as in the case of the misogynous tales which the Wife of Bath represents as the learned literary gleanings of her late fifth husband.

How shall we read Jankyn's Book? Our first tasks, then, in the following chapters, are to reexamine the medieval Chaucer, and then to see what was claimed by his heirs.

## "SOURCES": TRANSLATION, PARODY, AND CONCEALMENT

Claiming and naming of ancestors evidently depend upon what is wanted by the inheritor, who discovers meanings in a given tradition for his own acknowledged or unconscious purpose. In 1555, Michelangelo carved the Pietà he intended for his own tomb out of a fragment of a fallen pediment from the Temple of Victory, as a last measure of his own achievement. In the marble lies a symbolic metamorphosis, from Greek original to pagan Roman copy to Florentine Christian triumph. Ideally, literary history should study the reflexive relations in which the present openly or subtly alters the past, in newly perceived hierarchies, readjusted values, as the modern is simultaneously transformed by the past in the process of confrontation: Virgil in Dante, Dante and Virgil in Chaucer, all three simultaneously in Spenser. In such dialogue, whether or not names are used or allusions suppressed, there is adversary relationship. The colloquies of poets perhaps rarely come close enough to the surface of consciousness to be recognized, and the recognition of sources opens new horizons for misinterpretation, as hazardous as the indefinable limits of historical ignorance. For literature, as Wellek reminds us, has a temporal reality; it is a public artifact, and the poet has first a role, an audience, and social status in the real world. Attempts to describe his role and his audience soon reveal the poverty of criticism without history; but to describe the influence of the contemporary audience or the social milieu upon the poet is a task for the biographer. The roles of poet and audience and the history of ideas within the poem are not, in this sense, "historical," they are self-reflexive perspectives of the poem itself.

Like all works of art, ancient and modern, fictions have antecedent sources and histories, but only copyists—plagiarists and verbatim translators—can, with luck, be traced to their true originals in place and time. In 1345, Richard de Bury commented ironically on the fakery and deception practiced by his contemporaries, speaking as the voice of his "counterfeit" books, in the imagery of Renaissance "rebirth":

> What wonder is it then, if clerical apes magnify their margins from the works of authors who are dead, as while they are yet living they endeavor to seize upon their recent editions? Ah, how often do you pretend that we who are old are but just born, and attempt to call us sons, who are fathers? and to call that which brought you into clerical existence, the fabric of your own studies? In truth, we who now pretend to be Romans are evidently sprung from the Athenians... and we who are just born in England shall be born again tomorrow in Paris, and being thence carried on to Bologna, shall be allotted an Italian origin, unsupported by any consanguinity.

While the Southwark tavern in Chaucer's *Prologue* bears a strong and suggestive resemblance to an actual tavern known to the fourteenth-century London world of Chaucer's audience, the Tabard—like the Mermaid, and the Spouter Inn in New Bedford—requires no corroboration beyond what takes place in it. John Fisher speculates that Chaucer chose

> to assemble his pilgrims at the Tabard Inn, across from St. Mary Overys Priory in Southwark... as an acknowledgement that he was finally taking his departure from Gower's own metier, the vices and virtues and criticism of the estates.

But as the starting point for the fictional journey to Canterbury—to Becket's shrine, which the pilgrims never reach—the Tabard is a point of no return, like the Malvern Hills and Santa Maria Novella in Florence, although Boccaccio's three young men do, in fact, return the seven young ladies to the church where they had met, "and after taking leave of them went about their business." The *Decameron* aristocrats, Langland's Long Will, and Chaucer's thirty pilgrims belong to the same realm of symbolic reality, of the universal "I" and "you," as the eagles in the *Parliament of Fowls* and the *Book of Fame*. The true sources and "historicity" of a fiction can neither be verified nor proved false. Thus Macpherson's pseudomedieval "Ossian" (1760-63) and Chatterton's "gothick" "Elinoure and Juga" (1769) are authentic fictions, and the "Rowley" poems of 1777 truly reflect the Gothic enthusiasm of the eighteenth century—a literary society apparently outraged by the printing of Urry's *Chaucer* (1721) in Roman type rather than black letter, but delighted to be deceived by "Gamelyn" *Shamela*, Pope, and Gay. Cultural history and the recovery of probable sources enlarge our conception of meaning and reduce the margin of error in interpretation, but they are rarely more than probable, nor are the most striking analogues ever a perfect match. Chance parallels are rarer than imitations, but even red herrings are valuable in the study of sources, influence, "evolution."

Homage that is truly disinterested is even more rare. No poet ever alludes to another great name, or names himself, inadvertently. Chaucer's naming of himself and his *auctors* provides a paradigm for "authority" at the beginning of the new tradition in English poetry to which all succeeding generations looked back. The later naming of Chaucer with epithets, as "English Homer," "Dan Geffrey," "Tityrus," like the silent imitations he practiced himself, became a means for an English poet to define himself against what had been done before. Naming him is sometimes merely formulaic apostrophe, but occasionally, as in Milton, significant invocation. Even the humble younger Lydgate, adding his *Siege of Thebes* to the *Canterbury Tales*, attempts to maintain his independence in the immediate context of his powerful master. One of Lydgate's modern defenders, Alan Renoir, declares that even though the tale pays homage to Lydgate's *maister* Chaucer, as in a scholar's Festschrift,

> it allowed him to put a new twist on his favorite topos [affected modesty], . . . [yet] his borrowing was free from the tyranny of a specific model whose example must be constantly followed.

Imitative adaptation and transformation of traditional styles and forms occur commonly in all the arts, beginning with elementary exercises in copying, ending in mastery; out of imitation comes the mutagenesis of new form. Picasso made dozens of studies of Velasquez's "Las Meninas," modifying and playing with the planes of its imagery more than fifty times. Prokofiev's and Stravinsky's uses of Bach and Handel repeat the theme. As in the greatest poems of Pope, imitation is not merely parody or derivative burlesque, but art made new; the *Dunciad* is an appropriation of the epic, which tests the unique strengths of both model and imitator. In major artists, imitation is extension, recognized conquest; in lesser, we find minor exploits and fugitive explorations on a miniature scale. Chaucer, as a translator and borrower from first to last, wrote the first great "imitations" in English poetry; he then in turn became the subject of imitation, conscious and unconscious, by his immediate heirs and their later successors. The study of *Troilus and Criseyde* reveals both dimensions of Chaucerian imitation: it is the epitome of his own synthetic fiction making, and it became a model, in the Renaissance evolution of the poem, marvellously transformed.

## RENAISSANCE PERSPECTIVE: CHAUCER AND THE *OLDE BOOKES*

From Lydgate to Spenser, English poetry acquires a new sense of its own historicity. The word *modern*, apparently first used by Dunbar circa 1520, comes into common use, as distinct from "ancient," in the 1580's. Of course, the concept (*moderna*, from *modo*) belongs to every age, as the sense of *now*. Increasingly remote and finally, as England's historic national literature, distinct from the older antiquities (Roman, then Greek), the poetry of the Christian Middle Ages grew to be an increasingly problematic legacy for the later English poets who inherited all traditions and compared their state with their continental rivals' in the last permutations of the Renaissance. Chaucer, Langland, and Gower, then finally Chaucer alone, became, posthumously, progenitors. As Shakespeare's "Gower" says,

> The purchase is to make men glorious;
> Et bonum quo antiquius, eo melius.

*Pericles* (1607-08) is probably the first of Shakespeare's Jacobean romances, and in its choral Prologue, "Gower" renews the medieval devices that conventionally mark departure into fantasy: "I tell you what mine authors say"(1. 1. 20) (*myn auctor seyth . . .*):

> To sing a song that old was sung,
> From ashes ancient Gower is come;
> Assuming man's infirmities,
> To glad your ear, and please your eyes.
> It hath been sung at festivals,
> On ember-eves and holy-ales
> And lords and ladies in their lives
> Have read it for restoratives.
> [1. 1. 1-8]

After Speght's two editions of Chaucer's *Works* in 1598 and 1602, no new edition was called for for eighty-five years. The poems of Gower, printed by Berthelette in 1533 and reprinted in 1554, were not edited again until 1857. The great medievals, as Lounsbury remarked, had become ancestral poets, whom it was respectable to name but no longer essential to read.

Reflecting on his own consciousness of time in his *Account of the Greatest English Poets* (1694), Addison uses a typical Augustan metaphor of "rust" for the medieval past, echoing Shakespeare's "ashes":

> Long had our dull Forefathers slept supine
> Nor felt the Raptures of the Tunefull Nine
> Till Chaucer first, a merry Bard, arose;
> And many a story told in Rhime and Prose.
> But Age has rusted what the Poet writ,
> Worn out his language and obscur'd his Wit.
> In Vain he jests in his unpolish'd strain
> And tries to make his Readers laugh in vain.
>
> [9-16]

Six years later, Dryden published his great "Preface to the Fables" and translations, thus setting Chaucer, newly "restored," back again next to Virgil and Ovid. Rust, of course, means the metamorphosis of matter by the transformation of energy in slow fire. What Addison wanted in his common-place is the negative effect of this process, solidity and clear form turning to shapeless dust, the illegible epitaph. The universality of such clichés for medieval antiquity—but not the "classic" past—"wasted," "crumbling," "decayed," "barbarous"—reveals the poetic imagination recoiling in fear of its own disintegration. What is the power of the word, which cannot be saved, nor save itself? The terrible gothic darkness of the age that ends Pope's *Dunciad*,

> Lo! thy dread Empire, Chaos, is restor'd;
> Light dies before thy uncreating Word:
> Thy hand, great Anarch! lets the curtain fall;
> And Universal Darkness buries all,

is no bleaker than that in Chaucer's satire on the confusion of tongues in his own, in *The Former Age*:

> Yit was not Jupiter the likerous,
> That first was fader of delicacye
> Come in this world; ne Nembrot, desirous
> To regne, had nat maad his toures hye,
> Allas, allas! now may men wepe and crye!
> For in oure dayes nis but covetyse,
> Doublenesse and tresoun, and envye,
> Poyson, manslauhtre, and mordre in sondry wyse.
>
> [56-63]

The mutability of language is a latent element in all interpretations of medieval poems, where the theme of anxiety is consciously struck again and again in the *translatio regni, memento mori,* and *ubi sunt* formulae, lamenting the past and the dead, even in seriocomic execrations of careless scribes. The reader of the Renaissance Chaucer confronts the formulae in the context of increasing linguistic obsolescence and textual obscurity in the early editions of Chaucer's poems. Chaucer's book, now an *olde boke*, is the source of both

Elizabethan reverence and condescension toward the past, the theme of Chaucerian irony in the *Book of Fame*, where we first begin to see his own ambivalence toward *auctors*. It became a constant element in everything he wrote.

In the freedom of the Elizabethan stage, where the invisible *auctor* has vanished entirely, replaced by dramatis personae who act out the fiction, one of the problems of authority most relevant to Chaucer and Gower was solved:

> We commit no crime
> To use one language in each several clime
> Where our scenes seem to live. I do beseech you
> To learn of me, who stand in the gap to teach you.
> [*Pericles*, 4. 4. 6-10]

Here Shakespeare has "Gower, as Chorus" to stand in the gap, as well as the goddess Diana and pantomime: "What's dumb in show, I'll plain with speech." The task of narration, in the staging of Shakespeare's *Troilus and Cressida*, is reduced to the brief speech of the Prologue, whose exit symbolizes the disappearance of the omniscient Chaucerian narrator as the maker of the fiction. But for medieval poets, and for Spenser, the problems of *myn auctor*, the audience, and the fictitiousness of speech are entangled with the task of self-impersonation and the presentation of dramatis personae in actions which take place in the mind—in allegory, fable, romance. The study of the poetic influence of Chaucer in the Renaissance must first go back to the open questions of medieval poetry as a written, not oral, art, to the poem conceived to be read. *Allegoria* and *ironia* "intend" multiple meanings, but the interpretation of intention need not be arbitrary. In the metamorphosis of Chaucer from medieval to Renaissance lies the evolution of allegory itself, which became for Puttenham, in 1589, "dissimulacion," *False Semblant*. Chaucerian irony and his allegory demand close reading.

Many of the old ambiguities of the verb *to read*, Middle English *reden*, still remain alive. It means, in its oldest sense (OE *rǣdan*, *rēden*) 'the giving or taking of counsel,' 'to have or exercise control,' with the sense of considering or explaining something mysterious such as a dream or riddle. It can be used for *think, conjecture*, or *guess*. Spenser was the first to use it to mean 'foresee, foretell,' in 'to read one's fortune,' and he alone used it to mean, 'see, discern, distinguish.' He also used it as a substantive, meaning 'speech.' In Middle English, "to read" may mean to interpret, to peruse without uttering in speech (to scan or interpret in thought); to learn, by perusal of a book; to utter aloud and render in speech something written; to instruct, advise, or to teach. *Rede* is frequently a colorless variant for *say, tell*; it can mean 'to find mention or record of something,' or simply 'to rehearse,' 'speak,' or 'tell of a subject.' The *Lenvoy of Chaucer a Bukton* exploits a range of the ambiguities of *rede* and a written text which suggests almost everything there is to be said about "reading a fiction" and the meaning of *auctoritee*, yet the poem leaves all, characteristically, in doubt. Shall Bukton risk marriage, or not? Chaucer is asked to "advise":

> This lytel writ, proverbes, or figure
> I sende yow, take kepe of yt, I rede;
> Unwyse is he that kan no wele endure.
> If thow be siker, put the nat in drede.
> The Wyf of Bathe I pray yow that ye rede
> Of this matere that we have on honde.
> God graunt yow your lyf frely to lede
> In fredam; for ful hard is to be bonde.
>
> [25-32]

"If you are secure, don't put yourself in doubt: 'read' the Wife of Bath. *Yf that hooly writ may nat suffyse, / Experience shal the teche*; as for myself, I say nothing at all." It is this Socratic Chaucer and his subtlety and autonomy—a master, posing as a servant of rhetorical conventions—which are most vulnerable to the mutability and disintegration of language, in his evolution to "antiquity" in the Renaissance.

## THE APOLOGY FOR FICTION: CHAUCERIAN AND SOCRATIC IRONY

Why, one asks, was Chaucer the only medieval English poet still thought worth reading, and why was only he revived, imitated, and revered in the Renaissance? Because of his wit, his love poetry, his vividness as a social historian? In the short run, there are possible answers to such questions, but in the longer run they will not do. The premises are false, and the isolation of Chaucer is misleading. His prolific successor Lydgate, as we shall see, was widely read and admired, and his contemporaries Gower and Langland had, at least in the earlier period, as large an audience. Of the great medieval poets, however, only Langland is truly an Anglo-Saxon original; Chaucer and Gower are chiefly poetic translators. Gower's major works are in three languages: Latin, French, and English, while Chaucer worked from Latin, French, and Italian into English. Chaucer's distinctive achievements as a poet are to be found in his discoveries of means of concealment of himself, of art that seems to be artless. These are certainly not the qualities he was praised for by contemporaries, nor did the Elizabethan writers who looked back to him consider him a master of simplicity. To his fifteenth-century heirs, he was the epitome of elegance, Dunbar's "rose of rhetoricians." Spenser, Sidney, and Shakespeare saw him as a primitive genius, admirably learned for a barbarous time, handicapped by the very crudeness of his medium in an age ignorant of great art.

All three of the great Middle English poets, Chaucer, Gower, and Langland, were regarded by their contemporaries and descendants as moralists who wrote according to the universal sanction for poetry, sacred and profane: *movere et docere; docere et delectare*. Yet it seems to me that, unlike Gower and Langland, Chaucer alone used poetry as a mode of inquiry as well as of instruction and delight. Unlike his contemporaries', his poems are difficult to reduce to moral statements, although he begins with the same moral premises and assumes a similar religious context. Chaucerian allegory and Chaucerian irony and ambiguity are unique and distinct from Gower's and Langland's kinds of allegory and irony. At a distance, the frameworks in which all three begin are common and "typically medieval": we find the familiar dream and the dream landscape opening up to be ready symbolically according to cues placed by the narrator, which follow conventional codes external to the poem and may be taken for granted by the audience. The interpretation of the poem is set in motion and conducted by the narrator, who leads the audience toward their goal. It is here, however, that questions arise, far more frequently in Chaucer than in any other medieval poet. In virtually every other poet, answers can be found for difficult questions of intention; in Chaucer's poems, nothing can be taken at face value, and certainty is rarely possible. The uniquely Chaucerian quality, in the dream visions, the *Canterbury Tales*, and most profoundly in *Troilus and Criseyde*, is the uncertainty of the narrator as to what his poem means. He is led, rather than leader; he follows, and he is almost always in doubt.

Chaucer's discoveries as a poet, and his originality, lie not in narrative—plots, myth making, invention—but in voices, and in the controlling of language so that voices other than his own are made to speak. . . . As a translator of extraordinary range, he brought a wealth of new kinds of poetry into English; but so, of course, did Gower. As a moralist and ironist, he explored the world he lived in and exposed its hypocrisy and vice; but so, too, did Langland. More than either of them, or any other medieval poet, however, he questioned the worth of his own art, the ambiguity of language, and the pretensions of poets to know or say more than other men. It is a very ancient ploy to remain ambivalent as to one's capacity to speak, and Chaucer alone among his medieval contemporaries mastered the rhetoric of ambiguity.

I shall frequently find reason, in reading Chaucer in the Middle Ages and in the Renaissance, to turn to Plato. The Platonism that grew and flourished in twelfth-century France provided medieval poetry with a new world of allegorical imagery and cast the poet in a new philosophical role. The higher Platonism of the Renaissance immensely magnified that role, with the adding of the *Symposium*, the *Phaedrus*, and the *Ion* to the medieval *Timaeus* as texts to justify the visionary imagination. The question of poetry in Plato, in the earlier Middle Ages, arises in a dialogue perhaps as well known in medieval Europe as it was in the sixteenth century, and as indispensable to both: the *Phaedo*, Socrates' argument for the immortality of the soul. The *Phaedo* also recounts the last days in prison of Socrates, while he awaited the end of Apollo's festival, for which his execution had been postponed.

The relevance of the *Phaedo* for medieval poetry is, I think, very clear from the opening episode on; the subject there raised is whether or not death is to be feared. Plato begins obliquely, with Socrates' release from the chains on his legs, and leads from the subject of pleasure and pain into the myth of the afterlife, the soul's escape, and its following of its guide or *daimon* beyond Hades into the other world. The dialogue concludes with Socrates drinking the hemlock. The portion of the dialectic that is most interesting for the present study is its introduction, the means Plato uses to shift the focus from the immediate state of the body to the survival of the mind, and Socrates' conception of eternity.

Cebes interrupts a remark of Socrates on the double nature of pleasure and pain to ask him if the rumor is true that he has been writing poems, "putting into verse stories of Aesop and composing a hymn to Apollo." No one has ever heard of him doing such a thing before, and his mocking opinion of the rhapsodes is well known. Socrates' reply amplifies what he said at his trial, about the voice of his *daimon*:

> I was trying to discover the meaning of some dreams, and I wrote the poems to clear my conscience, in case this was the sort of art that I was told to pursue. It happened something like this: the same dream had kept on coming to me from time to time throughout my life, taking different forms at different times, but always saying the same thing: "Socrates, pursue the arts, and work hard at them." I formerly used to suppose that it was urging me to do what I was in fact doing, and trying to encourage me in the performance of that: that like those who shout encouragement to runners in a race, so the dream, when it urged me to (*mousiké*) pursue the arts, was encouraging me in what I was doing; for philosophy is the greatest of all arts, and that was my pursuit. But then when the trial took place, and the god's festival prevented my execution, I thought that just in case the dream meant, after all, that I should follow this popular kind of art, I ought to follow it and not disobey. It seemed safer not to depart before salving my conscience, by the composition of poems in obedience to the dream. So I first wrote in honor of the god for whom the ceremonies were being held, and then, after the hymn, realizing that the "poet," if he was going to be a poet or composer at all, must compose not fact but fiction, and that I myself was not a story teller, I used fables that were ready at hand—the fables of Aesop, which I knew—the first of them I came across.

The speech ends with Socrates' farewell message to Evenus, the poet: "Tell him, if he has any sense, to follow me as quickly as he can."

While Boethius and Prudentius are the primary medieval sources for the sacred dream and its allegory, the older pagan forms also survive, and invite speculation. What this Socratic defense provides, then, is Plato's testimony as to the visionary voice in dreams and the two fundamental modes of poetry, the sacred hymn and the "fiction"—the fable that does not have to be true in order to be delightful, that can be invented on the spot, translated, or made to mean anything at all, since it is "composed," a fable. Socrates makes a clear distinction between storytelling as an art and the voice of the *daimon* in his dream, just as he distinguishes between sacred and secular poetry. When he needs myth—or Homer—in order to describe "the shape of the earth as I believe it to be," it is a story. "As Homer describes it," we see the underworld of Hades and its four rivers, and the "pure dwelling place up above" for those who are released "from these regions and depart from them as from a prison"; the cosmic image is made visible by Socrates' imagination. He has the power to envisage and describe it, but as to its truth, he cannot go beyond hope and the risk a rational mind is willing to take:

> No man of sense should affirm decisively that all this is exactly as I have described it. But that the nature of the souls and their habitations is either as I have described, or very similar, . . . that, I think, is a very proper belief to hold, and such as a man should risk, for the risk is well worth while. And one should repeat these things over and over again to oneself, like a charm, which is precisely why I have spent so long explaining the story now.

Interpretation of Chaucers' dream-vision poetry properly begins with Boethius. However, the survival of Socrates' *daimon*, his irony, and his ambivalence toward fiction making, in the dialogues of the medieval Platonic tradition, the *Timaeus*, *Meno*, *Phaedo*, and the *Apology*, provide a deeper perspective for criticism than the Christian exegetes, rhetoricians, and the literary sources, named and unnamed, we now know he knew. We shall approach the medieval Chaucer indirectly, through Spenser and the Elizabethan defense of allegory, and then through the ending of the *Book of Fame*, the most enigmatic of his visionary poems, because it focuses on the art of poetry, and on the poet. It would seem to me to yield something more of its eccentricity to an oblique approach, through the ambiguous Neoplatonic figure of Genius the poet, than through the traditional study of its *auctors*, the heterogeneous mélange of Virgil and Dante, Alan de Lille and Jean de Meung, medieval science and the texts of *artes poeticae*. All of these are present (as elsewhere in his poems), and all too visible. But the issues the poem confronts are those which its narrator evades, and they suggest risks he was not willing to take. The *Book of Fame* is, I think, Chaucer's most Socratic poem, and its treatment of *auctoritees* suggests the central problems we face in interpreting Chaucerian irony, which grow deeper in the other stories he found, "fables ready at hand," for the poet, "if he is to be a poet at all, must compose not fact but fiction."

DONALD R. HOWARD

# The Idea of "The Canterbury Tales"

## THE NARRATIVE NOW

In the *Troilus*, as in *The Canterbury Tales*, time moves forward from Creation to Doomsday and the past is a sequence of unique events. But in the *Troilus* these events are selected because of their historical and moral meaning. The story of Troilus is told because Troy's fall brought the founding of the West and because Troilus reveals a type of earthly striving in which the reader is able to divine a moral meaning. In addition the story of such a hero, who died honorably in a decisive battle, is told to preserve his name and reputation, to establish in the successive stream of human lives the "glory" which medieval knights deemed a just reward for noble deeds. Thus everything specific and historical in this style gets its profoundest meaning from what it shares with other unique events; the events of the *Troilus* happen in a span of three years, but their meaning is the same as that of any passing love or any fallen city. Troilus sees this meaning at the end when he is removed from time. From such a point of view the unique historical event is one in a series of endless repetitions. This repetitive quality in human experience invites the author to associate events with the repetitions of seasonal change: Troilus's experience of three years is equated in the poem's imagery with a single revolution of the seasons and with the turning of Fortune's wheel.

*The Canterbury Tales* has no such pattern. It depicts a one-way journey. There is no suggestion in the Parson's Prologue that a new day will dawn, or that the pilgrims will turn about and go home. We part from them at a "thropes ende" beyond Harbledown on the Canterbury Way, probably the

From *The Idea of The Canterbury Tales*. Copyright © 1976 by the Regents of the University of California. The University of California Press, 1976.

place where pilgrims first caught sight of the cathedral and dismounted to praise God. The journey is allegorized as the "parfit glorious pilgrimage / That highte Jerusalem celestial." Nothing happens here which has happened before. In the last fragments there are no repeated lines or backward references. The unexpected arrival of the Canon's Yeoman suggests rather the random and unpredictable quality of events as they follow in sequence, and his tale introduces a new kind of subject. Everything moves on, nothing is finished. The sun casts long shadows; the moon rises into Libra, a symbol of justice. The Host's ordinance is "almost fulfilled"; he says all tales have been told but one. It is 4 P.M., the "eleventh hour." Nor in the tales themselves do we ever go over the same ground twice—each tale is a new beginning. Often, it is true, the tales look back to previous tales in a parodic or ironic or disputatious spirit, but this looking back always adds something new, makes a reply, sees things in a different light. We never get the feeling, as we do at the end of the *Troilus*, that we are back where we started, that *plus ça change plus c'est la même chose*.

As we pass along in the linear sequence of *The Canterbury Tales*, each experience of the pilgrimage—each person, each interchange, each tale— has a momentary interest which makes it *seem* to happen in the present. If we imagine the present moment—"now"—as a moving dot between the remembered past and the unknown future, this "now" in *The Canterbury Tales* is simply our continued experience of reading or hearing the work; the dot moves along the span of time during which the narrator describes the pilgrimage incident by incident and tale by tale. Into this linear performance the tales introduce events of various past times and various places—a "then" which was once "now," and which becomes "now" again in the telling. This is altogether different from *Troilus and Criseyde*, in which Chaucer portrayed a *distant* past: acknowledging that "in sundry ages,/ In sundry londes, sundry been usages" (II:27-28), he deliberately dwelt upon the strangeness and distance of ancient Troy. As he drew close to the most intimate scenes (in Book II) he invoked the muse of history. He depicted an ancient, doomed city in the last days before its fall, represented its pagan rites and philosophies, showed its people moving haplessly in intellectual and spiritual darkness. He described that world with scenes and language of fourteenth-century England, but he used this anachronism intentionally to create an impression of immediacy and reality. He was aware that "in form of speche is chaunge / Within a thousand yeer," and that words which then meant something "now wonder nice and straunge / Us thinketh hem" (II:22-24), so he translated their words and actions into modern equivalents. There is nothing "naive" about this—it does not betray a defective "sense of the past": it is used for artistic effect, to make vivid and understandable a pre-Christian culture. When the poet wanted he could make Trojan life appear so familiar that it seemed to be happening before our eyes; but no less often he put that world at a historical distance, playing up its strangeness.

In *The Canterbury Tales* Chaucer abandoned this technique. He brings the past momentarily into the present, flattens out foreignness and distance in time. All the scenes of the actual pilgrimage, in the General Prologue and the various prologues and links, are recounted in the simple past: "At night *was come* into that hostelrye. . . ." "A knight there *was*. . . ." "With him there *was* his son, a young Squier. . . ." Whatever else we need to know is related as anterior: "thereto *hadde he riden*. . ."; "he *hadde been* sometime in chyvachie." The "historical present" is never used for the events of the pilgrimage itself. "Greet chiere *made* our Host," we learn. "Our conseil *was* nat longe for to seche"; "This thing *was* graunted"; "Amorrowe . . . up *rose* oure Host"; the Knight "*bigan* . . . His tale anon. . . ." These events, when done, pass into anterior time:

> Whan that the Knight *had* thus his tale *ytold*,
> In all the route *nas* there young ne old
> That he ne said it *was* a noble storie.
> (I:3109-3111)

Chaucer does not say "it had been" a noble story; the stories themselves are not placed in anterior time once told, but are permitted to come up into the present and remain there, preserved in memory, tradition, or writing, able to be told again. Events are bound to time (and telling or hearing a tale is an event), but a tale has a life of its own—it lives in the pseudoeternity of tradition and reputation, in the house of Fame. The present tense is thus used for the immediate moment in tale-telling, the moment of direct communication between teller and listener. For example, we learn of the Friar,

> He *was* an esy man to yeve penaunce
> Ther as he *wiste* to have a good pitaunce.
> For unto a povre ordre for to yive
> *Is* signe that a man is well yshrive.
> (223-226)

The narrator reports the Friar's words or thoughts in the present tense, as if the Friar were saying it himself or Chaucer the pilgrim repeating it and expecting us to agree. The present tense is the moment of participation, the moment when a thing that *was* is passed from one brain to another in the mutual act of communication. Thus the narrator says, speaking of the Monk, "And I *said* his opinion was good": his agreement with the Monk is presented as an event which took place on the pilgrimage. But then he lapses into the present: "What sholde he study . . . ? How shall the world be served?" We get a little monologue—a thought, as it actually is—which has passed from the

Monk's mind to the narrator's and now passes from the narrator's to ours. Then we return to past events: "Therefore he *was* a prikasour. . . ." In the same way Chaucer says of the Summoner's Latin "No wonder *is*, he herd it all the day," and goes on

> And eek ye *knowen* well how that a jay
> Can clepen "Watte". . . .
> (642-643)

In a moment he will lapse from the present tense back to the past:

> But now *is* time to you for to telle
> How that we *baren* us that ilke night,
> Whan we *were* in that hostelry alight;
> And after *wol I tell* of our viage. . . .
> (720-723)

This "now" has for its future the narrator's stated intentions and expectations. He includes us, the audience, in the ongoing action, lets us know what we can expect.

This circumstance—that we are present *in the work* as hearers or readers—is expressed in a passage whose temporal relationships are remarkable:

> The Miller *is* a cherl, ye know well this;
> So *was* the Reeve eek and othere mo,
> And harlotrie they tolden bothe two.
> Aviseth you, and put me out of blame;
> And eek men *shall* nat make ernest of game.
> (I:3182-3186)

Why in these lines is the past tense used of the Reeve, the present tense of the Miller?—because the Miller is there at hand about to tell his tale. It is as if the narrator were watching with us. What he remembers from the past he can promise for the future—both "tolden" harlotry. But he states this in the past tense as a fact, not in the future tense as an expectation. Addressing us parenthetically, he removes (so to speak) the mask of the Miller, which he is about to put on again—holds the mask at arm's length as he pauses to comment. It is one of the most extraordinary moments in medieval literature: "Aviseth you," he tells us—think it over, make up your minds. And then he makes up our minds for us: "Men *shall* nat make ernest of game." Like the Host, who had the company hold up their hands in assent before they knew what they were assenting to, he tells us to respond freely and then tells us how to respond!

All the double truths we must accept are present in this passage: the voice addressing us is at once the poet who writes and the narrator who rehearses; the narrator is at once teller and performer; the pilgrims are at once being performed and performing; we the audience are at once hearers and readers; and we are free to choose but told how to react. The present moment in the General Prologue and in the links between tales is precisely the moment when all these paradoxes are held in balance—the moment when we are paying attention and are successfully in communication with the narrator as he tells or "rehearses." Hence the pilgrims' voices have the same ring of vivid direct communication as the narrator's. This is most evident in the prologues to tales: what personal presence in all literature is more immediate than the Wife or the Pardoner in their prologues? But it is notable in most of the tales as well. The pilgrims address us directly in the here and now: "This duke," says the Knight, "of whom I make mencioun, / Whan he was comen almost to the town. . . ." And the duke is thus recreated in the present by the Knight's "mencioun."

The narrator's voice helps create this sense of immediacy. Rarely does it emerge through the voice of the performing pilgrim, and at that in the most innocuous way—for example, in the Prioress's apostrophe: "Now maystow singen, follwing ever in oon / The white Lamb celestial—*quod she . . .*" (VII:580-581). At the end of the Pardoner's Tale, it is true, the narrator's voice recounts the squabble and the peacemaking that follows; but the voice is so gentle, and so solemn, that it is hard not to hear in it Chaucer's own. Chaucer's *own* voice intervenes constantly; it is one of the striking, and original, marks of the style. In the Knight's Tale we get many overtones of the poet's presence. The precedent is set there. But as often as not it is ambiguous: we have to decide for ourselves whether, say, at the end of the Nun's Priest's Tale the simple ironic moral is the priest's words or Chaucer's own, or both. One characteristic of the style is that we are often not able to tell what voice we hear and are not meant to.

This intervention of the poet's voice is comparable to the narrator's "interruptions" in the *Troilus*; but in the *Troilus* the narrator's direct address to the audience created distance, reminding us that he and we exist in the here and now, centuries later than the time of the story. In *The Canterbury Tales* there is no such contrast. Direct address by the poet or narrator never "distances" the story; it always achieves immediacy. The narrative present— the "now" we listen in—gives contemporaneity to the "then" of the story, never pushes it into the long ago or the far away.

If we could find any exception to this we would find it in the Knight's Tale. Like the *Troilus* it is adapted from a work by Boccaccio, is set in the ancient world, and is a tale of knightly deeds and courtly love. Like the *Troilus* it has a narrator (the Knight) who addresses us about the difficulty of his task: "I have, God wot, a large feeld to ere, / And wayke been the oxen in my plough" (886-887). But unlike the *Troilus*, this narrator is not explicitly identified with the author. Instead there emerges a voice who talks about writing (1201); for example, it asks about Palamon's imprisonment "Who coude rime in English proprely / His martyrdom?"—and then answers "for sooth it am nat I" (1459f). How or why this voice gets into the tale is a problem we will put aside for a later chapter. No one denies it is there. No one, I think, is any longer so bent on realism in *The Canterbury Tales* as to suppose that such a passage is the Knight's own words. Assuming then that it is an intrusive voice (Chaucer's own), what is its effect? Does it "distance" the story, remind us of its pastness and remoteness by bringing us momentarily back into the present? Can it for example be reckoned comparable in its effect to the following interruption in the *Troilus*, which occurs as the lovers embrace for the first time?

> What might or may the sely larke saye,
> Whan that the sperhauk hath it in his foot?
> I kan namore but of thise ilke twaye—
> To whom this tale sucre be or soot,
> Though that I tarry a yeer, somtime I moot,
> After myn auctour, tellen hir gladnesse,
> As well as I have told hir hevinesse.
>                                    (III:1191-1197)

I think that it cannot. The interruption in the *Troilus* just quoted has a dramatic value. In a moment of heightened intensity it draws the reader away, puts esthetic and historical distance between us and the lovers; to the extent that it is funny it can be compared with "comic relief." Its purpose is to draw us back, let us get our breath. The passage in the Knight's Tale is different. It is not an interruption; it comes at a moment of transition. The poet has just told how Arcite returned to Athens in disguise. "And in this blisse," he says, "let I now Arcite, / And speke I wol of Palamon a lite" (1449-1450). Then follow eight woeful lines about Palamon's long imprisonment, ending with the statement (in the present tense) that

> . . . he is a prisoner
> Perpetuelly, noght only for a yeer.

No sooner has this lame rime hobbled past than we get the question,

> Who coude rime in English proprely
> His martyrdom? for sooth it am nat I.
> Therefore I pass as lightly as I may.

Then the teller continues:

> It fell that in the seventh yeer, of May
> The thridde night (as olde bookes seyn,
> That all this story tellen more pleyn). . . .

This fleeting glimpse of a narrator searching old books clearer than his own and hurrying on does not at all create a momentary "distance" or "relief." On the contrary, it renders dramatically the very act which gives the Knight's Tale its immediacy and excitement—the act of drawing events from the recorded past into the narrative now.

How intensely this effect works in the Knight's Tale is best illustrated in its major scenes—the descriptions of the temples in Part III, the prayers, the battle, and the death of Arcite. Throughout there is constantly present an "I" who hovers over the story, representing himself as having been an eyewitness to the events:

> There saugh I Dane, yturned til a tree,
> I mene nat the goddesse Diane,
> But Penneus doghter, which that highte Dane.
> There saugh I Attheon an hert ymaked,
> For vengeaunce that he saugh Diane al naked;
> I saugh how that his houndes have him caught
> And freeten him, for that they knew him naught.
> Yet peinted was a litel further moor
> How Atthalante hunted the wild boor,
> And Meleagre, and many another mo,
> For which Diane wroght him care and wo.
> There saugh I many another wonder storie,
> The which me list nat drawn to memorie.
>                                    (2062-2074)

This "I" has actually *seen* the stories painted on the temple's wall, seen them with the kind of understanding which permits him to warn us like a school-master against confusing Dane and Diane. He claims, then, to be producing the stories out of memory, out of personal experience. From any repesenta-tional point of view it is preposterous—neither Knight, narrator, or poet has been in ancient Athens. It is rhetoric. But it will not do to dismiss it as a conventional "device" of rhetoric: no rhetorical device ever existed without a purpose, and no poet worth the name ever used any device just because it was conventional. The purpose here is to achieve immediacy through a deliberate anachronism: the pastness of the events is obliterated, "then" drawn up into "now." Pagan temples and prayers are modernized by association with planets and their influences. The teller becomes an eyewitness, represents the re-corded past as the remembered past. It is akin to the deliberate anachronism of the *Troilus*, but the "I" in the Knight's Tale is a more spectral presence than the bookish narrator of the *Troilus*, and no book is involved; the preposterous truth-claim is that the teller was there.

As we approach the climactic scene, a medieval tournament, the events of the story come less and less to be reported in the past tense: we get the "historical present," a familiar bit of rhetoric which draws the past into the narrative "now" and makes it happen before our eyes. This is the case in

the famous description of the battle, where Chaucer astonishingly lapses into
an approximation of alliterative verse:

> The heraudes left hir pricking up and down;
> Now ringen trumpes loud and clarioun.
> There is namore to sayn, but west and est
> In goon the speres full sadly in arrest;
> In gooth the sharpe spore into the side.
> There seen men who can joust and who can ride;
> There shiveren shaftes upon sheeldes thicke.
> He feeleth thurgh the herte-spoon the pricke.
> Up springen speres twenty foot on highte;
> Out goon the swerdes as the silver brighte;
> The helmes they tohewen and toshrede;
> Out brest the blood with stierne stremes rede;
> With mighty maces the bones they tobreste.
> He thurgh the thickest of the throng gan threste.
> There stomblen steedes strong, and down gooth all.
>                                         (2599-2613)

In what follows, the teller of the tale hovers over events, scrutinizing them in
the present tense as if they were happening in the palms of his hands. Of
Arcite's victory: "Who sorrweth now but woeful Palamon" (2652). Of the
moment of triumph: "Anon there is a noise of peple bigunne" (2660); Arcite
"pricketh endelong the large place" (2678). Of Arcite's wound: "Swelleth
the brest of Arcite" (2743). Of his death: "Arcite is cold" (2815). Of the
aftermath: ". . . by length of certein yeres, / All stinted is the moorning and
the teeres / Of Greekes" (2967-2969). These uses of the present tense are
taken at random—there are scores of others. The tale never abandons the
past tense, which is used for events that advance the main lines of the story;
but toward the end it uses the present tense more and more often. The very
opposite technique was used in the *Troilus*: the ending actually stretched
distance in time and space. Criseyde was removed to the Greeks, Troilus to
the eighth sphere; we and the narrator were removed into the Christian
present and, from it, into contemplation of the Christian mysteries. But in
the Knight's Tale the ending collapses temporal distance. The closing sentence even couples the final outcome and the final blessing on the audience,
as if the speaker had his eye at once upon the characters of the story and the
company of his listeners or readers:

> Thus endeth Palamon and Emelye;
> And God save all this faire compaignye!

The Knight's Tale sets this "narrative now" in the reader's mind and
establishes it as a stylistic feature of the work. The appropriation of the distant
and past to the here and now does not give us, as the *Troilus* did, a picture of a

civilization long dead to which we draw up and then away, part of a cyclical process of rises and falls. The Knight's Tale, and *The Canterbury Tales* generally, give us instead a picture of time ticking away, one event following another, the recorded and the remembered past coming alive randomly in the narrative now, where we perceive them, and passing again into the storehouse of memory.

## OBSOLESCENCE AND THE SOCIAL FABRIC

Yet there is a difference between the way we perceive time and the way we experience it. We perceive time by conceptualizing in periods or ages or tenses; but we experience time in little things. Dust on a tabletop, cracked plates, and piles of unread books give us messages which clocks and calendars do not. We experience time in newness and oldness, sameness and difference, unpredictability, repetitions, gaps. In various works Chaucer rendered time by various such experiences. If time in *The Canterbury Tales* is perceived as a passing "now" which moves in a passing age and that age is the last of a series, we have a very intellectual (and medieval) perception of time. But this moving "now" is rendered dramatically by the experience of *obsolescence*.

By obsolescence I mean the experience of things not yet obsolete about which it is feasible to predict an end. Chaucer distinguishes it from "newfangleness" and from "old things." Obsolescence bears the marks of past and future, for in it we see the boundary of each. Chaucer says of the Monk that he "let olde thinges passe, / And held after the newe world the space": the Monk chooses between new and old. Obsolescence has the Janus-like quality of encapsulating past and future; it is for that reason the most intense manifestation of the present. To grasp obsolescence requires an immersion in one's own time and place, a sensitivity not just to fads and fashions but to all fluctuations of ideas, hopes, customs, perceptions, habits, usages, structures and relationships, people and things. A sense of obsolescence calls for the most delicate response to the changes and movements of these, and so requires an eye for detail and a gift of precise expression: obsolescence lurks in subtleties—in the uses and textures of things, in nuances of languages, in gestures, in attitudes. It is based on memory. In our own time (and our own country) we grasp obsolescence unerringly—it is something we have a sense of, as one is said to have a sense of humor, of direction, or of the past. Once out of our own culture or milieu our sense of obsolescence fails us, as our sense of humor may do.

Let me offer an example. In America, at least on the east coast of America at the time I write, railroad travel is obsolescent. It is still part of life and for many a necessity; new trains go on being manufactured and improvements go on being made. It is in no way obsolete—train travel is still taken for granted. But trains have lost all newfangledness; there is no more glamor in them—there is perhaps romance and nostalgia. A sure sign of obsolescence is the emergence of enthusiasts who want to preserve what is passing, study what is past, and forestall what is to come. Whenever a train makes its last run, it is filled with writers and cultists, cheered at every stop by well-wishers and sentimentalists. And this is because the *idea* of train travel is obsolescent; the reality exists as much as ever in some places, but people experience that reality differently. All the appurtenances which once seemed luxurious—the chair cars, the dining cars, the lounges and bars, the little rooms and "parlours" with their stuffed chairs and chrome and mirrors—came to seem worn and démodé. The conductors, once grand dignitaries with waistcoats and precise gold watches, became surly officials of a dispirited bureaucracy. The waiters and porters who once practiced their arts with proud grace became grubby, fumbling, and annoyed. Compare the crisp affability of airline stewardesses, all Cheshire smiles and golden voices. In fact trains travel faster and are better and safer than they were ten years ago; but they have lost their dignity and wonder.

There are really no obsolescent things, only obsolescent ideas, attitudes, and values. The obsolescence is in us. It is our notions and our feelings about a thing which make it obsolescent and finally obsolete. There are obsolescent heroes (the cowboy), institutions (the church), locales ("downtown"), social ranks (servant), jobs (shoeshine boy), manners (tipping one's hat); and of course obsolescent styles, ideals, and words. Obsolescence is not to be found in fads or fashions, things by nature short-lived which owe their very existence to newfangledness and timeliness. The garment which is already "out" by the time it is bought, the automobile designed to look old (and fall apart) next year, this season's fashionable tag-words, songs, plays, dances, theories of literature—all these are just the flotsam and jetsam of culture; their changing is itself part of a culture. Nothing can be obsolescent until it has been institutionalized, has enjoyed some measure of stability in the life of a society. A newspaper, a bibliography, or a dictionary may be *obsolete* the day it is published, but that does not make newspapers, bibliographies, or dictionaries obsolescent. As a part of culture they will only be obsolescent if there emerges—as some think there has—a real possibility that they will be replaced by electronic devices.

One sign of obsolescence is nostalgia; another is renewal. Nostalgia produces all kinds of efforts to force renewal upon obsolescent things. The "Metroliner," the fast train which now speeds between New York and Washington, seems a model of train travel—comfortable, clean, frequently on time. Its attendants adopt a cheerful manner—all politeness and efficiency. Of course the meals in one's seat, the solicitous voice over the loudspeaker, the forced cheer, the display of efficiency, reveal how the new train is modelled on the airplane—and this makes some nostalgic for the way trains used to be. But such renewals are a part of obsolescence. And for that reason, another feature of obsolescence is uncertainty. We are never sure whether the renewal will succeed. It is unpredictable. If we *knew* that trains would disappear we would begin to call them obsolete. But as I write, a new company is formed to take over passenger trains; an official proclaims a "new era."

Obsolescence is probably one of the most important ways we experience time: it is entwined with the particularities of daily life, with what we esteem, think, and do. Yet in the *Troilus*, for all its focus on the domestic realm, we do not find obsolescence. We are thrown back into a former age which we know *is going to* pass away. We are reminded of a fallen civilization which went before (Thebes). We get a vivid picture of the life of noblemen in the ancient city (very like that of medieval knights and ladies), are made to understand their customs and values. But we never get a sense of their customs and values passing away or of new ones taking their place. We sense that a catastrophe is to happen. We know from hindsight it *will* happen. But we observe no changes subtly taking place in people's minds or in their culture or society. Their world is doomed, but their way of life is stable and secure.

In *The Canterbury Tales*, as we are made to feel the immediacy, the contemporaneity of its setting, we do observe changes in thought, culture, and society; our sense of obsolescence is invoked. The opening lines of the General Prologue, with their high-flown literary conventions modelled on French poetry, embody an obsolescent style—or so it would have seemed to Chaucer, who had turned to other models. This style is abandoned at once, and except here and there within the tales we do not encounter it again. The theme of springtime in these lines suggests time passing, and people turn in this season to old customs and traditions; but precisely at the moment when the poet abandons the obsolescent style—"Bifell that in that seson on a day, / In Southwerk at the Tabard"—he reminds us that the pilgrimage is the familiar national one, that it begins in a tavern and in the disreputable suburb Southwark. Everyone agreed the institution of the pilgrimage was not what it had been in old times, and Chaucer, though he represents the pilgrimage in its ideal and symbolical form at the end, shows the pilgrims at the outset and along the way following an obsolescent custom "after the newe way." We see too, in the General Prologue, that their stations in life are changing, that the social structure and the culture itself are changing.

This difference between the *Troilus* and *The Canterbury Tales* occurs because the poems deal with different social classes. In the *Troilus* all the characters are (to adopt a modern British distinction) "royals" or "nobles." The only social-class difference to be found is that between the ranks of princes (to which Troilus belongs) and the lesser ranks of nobles (to which

Criseyde belongs). We never see anyone below this class. Imagine how altered the work would be if there were scenes where the servants gossipped, as in the novels of Ivy Compton-Burnett, about secrets happening "below stairs." Suppose we saw the "commons" reacting to events or participating in the affairs of the doomed city; suppose a duenna like the nurse in *Romeo and Juliet* were present, some character like the Wife of Bath; or suppose characters like the Miller or even the Physician or Man of Law had a part in the *Troilus*. In the Trojan "Parlement" a wrong decision is made because of the "noyse of peple" (IV:183), the "folk" (202); these are presumably the lower classes. But we do not hear them talk. They only make noise, and they are wrong. If we saw more than one social group we might see changes in the social fabric, but the limitation to the upper classes obscures obsolescence. At the seat of power life seems stable—even private life. A story set exclusively in Buckingham Palace or the White House might—like the *Troilus*—give us a sense of a nation about to collapse, but it would probably leave us in the dark about specific social and cultural developments. For this reason clothes (which reveal status and social roles) figure much less prominently in the *Troilus* than in *The Canterbury Tales*.

In this respect *The Canterbury Tales* was a departure in Chaucer's style. None of his earlier poems, except for the last scene in the *Parliament of Fowls*, had anything to do with differences in social class. Not that there weren't precedents—there was "class satire" of the kind Gower was writing, and the lower classes get into the Italian frame-narratives. But in *The Canterbury Tales* Chaucer presented social-class distinctions in such a way as to point up the disparity between what people thought and what they did—between the obsolescent idea of social class which his society held and the more complicated actuality of its gradations. In the General Prologue he suggests the Three Estates (Gower *named* them in his prologue); but he describes a variegated and mobile set of social distinctions or "degrees." And he sets the idea of their obsolescence in our minds with the Knight.

The Knight, of the lesser nobility, is an obsolescent hero, a "knight of the Cross." The battles in which he has participated stretch back forty years. The three lists in which he has engaged at Tramissene would have seemed old-fashioned in the 1380s, for proper wartime lists became less frequent as warfare and weaponry became more elaborate. During the period he has been on these crusading expeditions, the English kings were at war with France, and this makes him seem the more an idealist. His values are the old chivalric ones—"trouth," "honour," "freedom," "courteisie," the unwillingness to say "villeinye." That he is meant to be viewed as an obsolescent figure is underscored by the portrait of his son the Squire. While the father is a warrior for old causes, the son exemplifies the fads of courtly life—he is elaborately dressed, accomplished in various skills, full of stylish joy, "curteis," "lowly," "serviceable," a "lover." As a fledgling warrior he has "borne him well" on one campaign, the disreputable "crusade" waged in 1382-1383 against the French in Flanders, a scandal, as it actually was, on which unruly captains plundered the land. The Squire must not be thought foppish or degenerate; but the knighthood and chivalry to which he has been bred is shown in decline.

There is reason to say that chivalry was always in decline, because its ideals, which originated in the twelfth century, bore at first a religious stamp. The old ideal of a chaste, monklike knighthood devoted to the protection of Jerusalem pilgrims, and the ideal of a united Christian commonwealth in which European knighthood might join forces, conquer the Holy Land, and Christianize the Mohammedans, was pretty much tarnished by the four-teenth century. Chivalry was a wordly institution based on otherworldly ideals: it was inevitable that the ideals should be compromised, mingled with a feudal and courtly ideology inimical to the ascetic tenor of Christian morality. If we ask what were the motives of knights, we come up with conflicting ones. To do good, to do justice, to punish the wicked—that is one side of it. Conquest and booty were the other. And in some respects these were legitimate motives—St. Thomas allowed that the wicked do not have the right to own property. Their other motive was "glory." It is said that by the fifteenth century this had replaced the profit motive. St. Thomas tells us that glory is the just reward for virtuous deeds, but he warns against the love of glory for its own sake, which is "vainglory." If we may judge from Theseus's stirring speech on Arcite's death at the end of the Knight's Tale, the Knight himself is motivated by glory. How easily it turned to vanity, arrogance, and pride may be seen in any history or biography of the period (John of Gaunt's would not be an exception). Froissart's *Chronicles* furnish nostalgic pictures of contemporary knights who were noble and chivalric; but Froissart shows us, too, the vain, arrogant ones. Later, the idea of knightly glory became centered in the king and the nation—it became the *gloire* of Louis XIV's time and the "national pride" (now obsolescent) which keeps us at war to this day.

The Knight's ideals are directly related to pilgrimage: the crusades were meant *au fond* to secure Jerusalem for Christian pilgrims. And a pilgrim's purpose was to do penance and adore relics. By Chaucer's time any thoughtful man would have seen this complex of goals with a jaundiced eye. There was already a fearful dichotomy between Church and State, symbolized by the martyrdom of Becket (very much in the background of *The Canterbury Tales*). Pilgrimages were discredited, relics scandalously abused. In depicting the Squire whose first campaign was a national disgrace, in revealing the unruly mirth and spite of the pilgrims, in placing at the end of the General Prologue the startling figure of the Pardoner with his pigs' bones for relics, Chaucer was depicting cultural ideals and practices which had lost their luster.

Of the clerical group described in the General Prologue—the Prioress and her entourage, the Monk, and the Friar—Chaucer makes much the same observation that he makes of the Knight and Squire. They exemplify obsolescent styles of life based on obsolescent ideas and practices. All three reveal what was throughout the Middle Ages the fundamental flaw in the practice of the religious life, that its values and ideals were contaminated by secular—and chiefly aristocratic—ones. Laymen put a high value upon social status, upon the acquisition of property and wealth, upon sexual relations, love, and family. Members of religious orders were, by ancient tradition, expected to renounce these preoccupations—to renounce "the world"—in vows of obedience, poverty, and chastity. Yet the Prioress, Monk, and Friar are all class conscious. The Prioress "peyned hir to countrefete cheer / Of court"; the Monk is handsomely dressed, loves horses and "venerie"; the Friar is "curteis" and "lowly of service." Some amount of wealth was required for the indulgences of which they are guilty, so it is apparent that none follows anything remotely like voluntary poverty. In addition the Monk and Friar, it is broadly hinted, indulge their sexual appetites; the Prioress, "digne of reverence," directs her maternal feelings to little dogs, mice in traps, little children in stories. The abuses of the three mount in intensity—the Prioress's are peccadillos which have a certain charm, the Monk's are bold offenses against the heart of the tradition (he apparently violates all three of his vows), and the Friar's make a veritable compendium of the wrongs ascribed to friars in fourteenth-century attacks. For the most part their offenses are the traditional ones of reformist and complaint literature.

We see each of the three religious against a past implied or stated in the portrait itself. It is not clear whether the Prioress is the daughter of a noble house or, as seems more likely, from the *haute bourgeoisie* or the "gentry": one rather assumes that in the circles where high social rank was taken for granted such manners and bearing were second nature—a lady of such a background wouldn't need to "countrefete" them. Madame Eglentine, when she took up the religious life, brought with her the values and mannerisms of her "degree." Her facial features are stereotyped aristocratic ones; the rosary of coral with green gauds which she wears about her arm is a ladylike adornment; the last detail—the brooch of shining gold inscribed with a crowned "A" and the motto *Amor vincit omnia*—similarly expresses her compromise between religion and "gentilesse." The brooch could be a pilgrim's badge, or a medal of St. Mary, or a medallion struck at the marriage or coronation of Queen Anne. The ambiguity of its religious and secular significance is not an unusual aspect of medieval art and artifacts. It is gold, it is ornamental, and its ambiguity is carried out in its Latin motto. What is striking is that she *has* it, for it is in all probability a memento, and an elegant one, of some past occasion.

The past associated with the Monk and Friar is institutional and historical, that of the Benedictine and Franciscan traditions. Speaking of the Monk, Chaucer explicitly describes this obsolescence of "old things" and speaks of the emergence of a "new world" (173-188). The famous passage refers to the chief characteristics of the Benedictine rule—the cloistered life of prayer, manual labor, and study—and compares the Monk's bare-faced scorn for the restrictions of monastic regimen. His class-consciousness is emphasized: he is capable of being an abbot, is a "lord" (172, 200), a "prelate" (204). His interests are the perquisites of nobility: hunting, fine horses and dogs, rich clothing, fur, ornaments. The "fat swan" mentioned at the end of the portrait (his favorite roast), like the palfrey he rides, is suitable to a nobleman. His ostentatious manliness is the nobleman's demeanor. And of course it is implied that he has not left behind him the nobleman's adventuresome sexuality—the hunting, the "pricking," the hare, possibly the "swink" he will reserve for St. Augustine and the "lust" mentioned in line 192, the "love knot" of his elaborate pin, bear down heavily on this implication. Later, taunted by the Host as a "tredefowl aright," he is to adopt the stance of a scholar and reveal his taste for reading stories about the falls of famous and powerful men, a "humanistic" interest. Not only old and new ideas are put in juxtaposition here, but monastic and aristocratic cultures, religious and secular values, the solitary and worldly lives, and divine and humane letters.

The Friar similarly holds after the new world. His abuses suggest the ideals of the Franciscan order—poverty, begging, good works—and Chaucer underscores this with ironic thrusts: "Unto his ordre he was a noble post" (214); "He was the beste begger in his hous" (252), and so on. As one who is supposed to be at large in the world and do acts of charity, he elects to do only what is pleasure or "profit." And yet it is part of Chaucer's style to make us empathize with his way of life even while we recognize it as a prototype of abuses. One imagines him to be handsome and young: his white neck is said to be a sign of sensuality, but if it is like the fleur-de-lys it is smooth and soft (and aristocratic), and he is physically strong (239) and undeniably energetic. He too has an aristocratic air: he is "vertuous" (251). The Friar is to the Monk and Prioress somewhat as the Squire was to the Knight: emphasis is thrown upon superficial traits, upon his fashionableness and stylishness. It is no accident that Chaucer uses the same phrase of him that he used of the Squire: "Curteis he was and lowly of servis."

Of the "commons"—those who are not knights or clerks—we get a social hierarchy going as high as the prominent Sergeant at Law and as low as the five "rogues" described last in the General Prologue. The Yeoman and Plowman represent the old ideal: the Yeoman, a forester dressed in green, is the Knight's servant and wears a warlike costume; the Plowman is the

Parson's brother. The two idealized figures they are attached to represent the two dominant groups of medieval society, the nobles and the clergy. It is to be assumed that the Yeoman has accompanied the Knight on his crusading expeditions; but, as is often pointed out, the reference to his arrows and "mighty bow" reminds one of the yeoman archers' successful performance at Crécy (1346) and Poitiers (1356)—battles fought a generation before. The Plowman is not merely an idealized but a symbolical figure, drawn ultimately from commentaries on Eccles. 6:19 and 2 Tim. 2:6. That he is the brother of the idealized Parson suggests the twelfth-century ideal of clergy and laity laboring in accord. There is a kind of primitivism in the conception: his hard manual labor symbolizes the possibility that honest toil and charitable works can restore human dignity lost in the Fall. And plowing itself symbolized the good works a Christian might do; the frequent references in Scripture to plowing and sowing were so interpreted, as the references to reaping and harvesting were understood to signify judgment.

> A trewe swinker and a good was he,
> Living in pees and parfit charitee.
> God loved he best with all his hoole herte
> At alle times, though him gamed or smerte,
> And than his neighebor right as himselve.
> He wolde threshe, and therto dyke and delve,
> For Christes sake, for every povre wight,
> Withouten hire, if it lay in his might.
> His tithes payde he full fair and well,
> Both of his propre swink and his catel.
> (531-540)

Any reader of Chaucer who has looked down at the footnotes knows that agricultural laborers were at a premium in the late fourteenth century because the Black Death and subsequent plagues had wiped out over a third of the work force. Serfs demanded freedom and agricultural smallholders chafed against the old manorial impositions. Their discontent was constant, the Peasant's Revolt of 1381 being the most violent expression of it. In such a period it is not surprising that the "churls" behave in a cheeky way, as they do in The Canterbury Tales. So it is the more surprising to find a small tenant farmer like the Plowman living in peace and perfect charity without a trace of discontent. To the extent that he can be thought a reality rather than an ideal, he would indeed have seemed an anachronism.

These two obsolescent figures from the lower end of the social scale contrast with other commons who are in a dependent or servile state; the Reeve and Manciple, for example, live by their wits and attain a stealthy independence. The Cook, temporarily in the employ of the Guildsmen, is a revolting figure with his "mormal" caused by uncleanliness, heavy drinking, and lechery. He is not really a servant but a small businessman with his own shop (it is full of flies, the Host remarks). Where the Yeoman and Plowman are from a rural, agrarian society, the Cook and Manciple are from London, a mercantile center. But the Miller and Reeve, who come from the country and have agricultural occupations, are no less venal. In the background are social and cultural changes subtly taking place in Chaucer's time—the shift from an agrarian to a mercantile society, from a simple barter and money economy to a complex commercial and credit economy, from a feudal and baronial government to a centralized monarchy.

When Chaucer turns to the burghers in the General Prologue he puts the Merchant first, perhaps to typify the mercantile basis for the "rise" of this social group. The others are presented in a more or less descending order of rank: the Man of Law, the Franklin, the Guildsmen, the Shipman, the Physician, and the Wife. They share (again, the Shipman is an exception) a certain pretentiousness about their social status. With most of them this is tied to money, for money or property or professional competence, not inherited titles or land, was the basis of their newly won standing. The notion is introduced with the picture of the Merchant, "Sowning alway th' encrees of his winning" (274-275). We learn that his winning comes in part from profiting illegally on rates of exchange, and we learn "There wiste no wight that he was in dette." This line means just what it says: no one knew that he was in debt. The next line makes clear the thrust of the statement—"So estatly was he of his governaunce." It is not implied that he was or wasn't in debt but that he managed prudently to keep his financial state to himself; he puts up a good front. Five of the seven portraits which follow repeat the Merchant's concern for wealth and appearances. The ways the pilgrims express their interest in rank and wealth run down the social scale in a fugue of pretentions. The Man of Law is a "greet . . . purchasour" (318) of land; the Franklin is a "householdere, and that a greet" (339); the Guildsmen have "catel . . . ynogh and rente" (373); the Physician loves gold "in special," is slow to spend money, has saved what he earned in plague times (441-442); the Wife spends her money on clothes and travel. Money is after all something different to everyone. The Man of Law wants landed property, the Franklin a great house, the Guildsmen silver knives rather than brass, the Physician savings. As each has a ruling passion, each has a special way he or she wants to *seem*. The Man of Law is "war and wise," "discreet," "of greet reverence"—"he seemed swich," adds the narrator, "his wordes weren so wise"; a busy man, "he seemed bisier than he was." The Franklin wants to seem rich, hospitable, "gentle." He is "Epicurus owene son," a gourmet with a penchant for lavish and ostentatious entertainment. Later (V:673-694) we find that he is disappointed with his son, who has failed to learn the aristocratic "virtue" and "gentilesse" for which he overpraises the Squire. The five Guildsmen, lower in status, are more modest in their expectations.

Each of them "seemed," we learn, "a fair burgeys / To sitten in a yeldehall on a deys" (369-370). Their silver knives, it is said, reveal their status; they are well dressed and equipped, and have sufficient property and income—a matter of importance to their wives, who like to be called "Madame" and walk at the head of a procession. The Physician is remote and conservative—learned, skillful, cautious in his diet, thrifty, well dressed, and acquisitive. Of all the "middle-class" members, the Wife, a cloth-maker, ranks lowest; where the wives of the Guildsmen aspire to walk at the head of a procession in a "mantel royalliche ybore," she is content with (but insistent on) going up first to the offering in her parish church. But "seeming" is no less important to her than to the others—her dress is elaborate and of excellent quality, though possibly bizarre, overdone, and rather old-fashioned. Her hat is appropriate to the lower classes and her wimple appropriate to a married woman.

It is curious that these worldly and faddish burghers show themselves bound to the past in their choice of tales. Only the Shipman tells a tale that seems to happen in the present day. The Man of Law and the Physician, sententious figures who display their learning, tell idealized, moralistic tales set in the long ago and far away. The Wife and Franklin turn to old romances—theirs are the only tales which begin with the formula "in th'olde days" or "in hir dayes." Of course each selects or adapts the romance to his or her own viewpoint and purpose: it is in keeping with the Franklin's awe of "gentilesse" that he has committed a Breton lay to memory, in keeping with the Wife's roots in southwest England that she knows an Arthurian tale. Then, too, the Wife and Merchant are obsessed with their *own* pasts—the Merchant cannot shake out of his mind his disastrous marriage and dashed hopes; the Wife's thoughts trail back over her husbands, her youth, her "gossib," her mother, her childhood.

Why are these upwardly mobile pilgrims, the ones most taken up with "newfangleness," so taken up with the past? They share a desire to make a future for themselves—the Man of Law is building up landed estates, the Franklin has great expectations for his son, the Guildsmen's wives anticipate higher honors, the Wife of five husbands' schooling cries "Welcome the sixth." Their immersion in their own time leads them toward its deepest values, and these are rooted in the past. Their thoughts go to the counsels of the Church and the traditions of the nobles. In their society status came from what the hag in the Wife's tale calls "swich gentilesse / As is descended out of old richesse." They might all like to believe with the hag that "genterye / Is nat annexed to possessioun," that wisdom and moral probity confer status, but they all know that for them money does so. Each uses the past to express his own self-image or hopes or anxieties.

All this emphasis on class distinctions and class consciousness gives us a feel for the contemporaneity of the setting and a sense of social changes and individual conflicts, but does it make any difference in diction or usage, in style as it is normally conceived? We might—in sheer bulk—find more passages of high-flown rhetoric, more of the "high style," in the *Troilus*, but we could find a fair amount of this in *The Canterbury Tales*. The difference is that in the *Troilus* whatever there is of high style and epic pretentions is under control: it all comes from the narrator. In *The Canterbury Tales*, except for the opening sentence, high style turns up only in the tales, where it has a way of *losing* control: the Knight's high style is parodied, the Squire's does a pratfall, the Nun's Priest mocks the thing itself. The *Troilus*, though, is a domestic story. Battles and heroic deeds are pushed into the background; chitchat, dinner parties, and a love affair are kept in the foreground, so there is plenty of colloquial speech. When Pandarus enters Criseyde's chamber she cries "What! which way be ye comen, *benedicite*? (III:757). That is not the way Dido and Beatrice talk; it has more in common with the Host's "Abide, Robin, leeve brother." It is an imitation of the way people speak familiarly to each other. In the *Troilus* there are long scenes of dialogue in this colloquial style. And the narrator, too, as often as he speaks a poetic or rhetorical diction, can buttonhole the reader and lapse into the familiar style:

> I passe all that which chargeth nought to seye.
> What! God foryaf his deth, and she also
> Foryaf, and with her uncle gan to pleye,
> For other cause was there none than so.
>                               (1576-1579)

Still, all the characters in the *Troilus* are from the upper classes and the narrator is a scholar, so their colloquial language is upper-class or educated speech. We never hear rude folk talking "low" speech.

The Canterbury Tales does give us "rude folk"—pulls us right into their little worlds. Their speech may sound like lower-class dialect, but Chaucer only makes a token effort to reproduce this. He has the Reeve speak a few words in an East Anglian dialect, and has the Reeve's clerks speak a broad Northern. He lets the Wife babble in her back-fence manner ("But now, sire, lat me see, what I shall seyn? / A ha! by God, I have my tale again . . ."), but she certainly doesn't speak the dialect of Bath; and the Manciple really speaks rather like an educated person (unless perhaps he has picked up his masters' speech patterns, like the lowly butler with the dandy accent). Though the Cook, Host, and Miller *sound* as if they are speaking like ordinary folk, there is little linguistic realism in their speech. The Cook would have spoken gutter-talk, but what does he say to the Host when he is falling-down drunk? he says,

> So God my soule blesse,
> As there is fall on me swich hevinesse,
> Noot I nat why, that me were levere sleepe
> Than the beste gallon wine in Chepe.
>
> (IX:21-24)

There, for sure, is a well-formed sentence; it is no less grammatical and no less toney than the Franklin's remark,

> . . . by the Trinitee,
> I hadde lever than twenty pound worth lond,
> Though it right now were fallen in myn hond,
> He were a man of swich discrecioun
> As that ye ben!
>
> (V:682-686)

True, Chaucer gives the Man of Law a few legal phrases and has the Host swear often. But that is about as far as it goes. Count up dialect variants and vocabulary items and you have to conclude that the characters all speak in much the same way. And all speak in verse. But we *perceive* them as speaking differently: the Lawyer's or Franklin's discourse seems more elevated than the Host's or Cook's because the minute scrutiny of social degrees and social mobility makes us anticipate this and presume it. The author doesn't need to imitate differences in their speech but only to suggest it.

The matter is important because it is sometimes argued that the tales themselves are all in the same style. To an extent this is true: any passage from any tale shares characteristics which could be distinguished from the styles of other fourteenth-century writers. But isn't it true, too, that the Wife's discourse can be distinguished, at least in some characteristic particulars, from the Knight's or the Reeve's? If style cannot be separated from content, each pilgrim's choice of a tale already recommends a certain style appropriate to that choice. As we have tales within a tale, we have styles within a style. It is another instance in which Chaucer contrives to have it both ways. The Cook is the lowest in degree, but he is capable of saying,

> For sikerly a prentise revelour
> That haunteth dice, riot, or paramour,
> His maister shall it in his shoppe abye,
> Al have he no part of the minstralcye.
>
> (I:4391-4394)

The Knight is the highest in degree, and he has his kingly hero say,

> And whoso gruccheth ought, he dooth follye,
> And rebel is to Him that all may gye.
> And certeinly a man hath most honour

To dien in his excellence and flour,
Whan he is siker of his goode name.
(3045-3049)

Where is the stylistic difference between these utterances? Not in the lexicon or syntax or dialect. Both *are* in the same style. But because the sense of obsolescence and the attention to social degrees has been pressed upon us, we *suppose* these utterances to be different. The difference is a matter of content and of social milieu. It would not suit the Cook's "style" to observe, like Theseus,

... gladder ought his freend been of his deeth,
Whan with honour up yolden is his breeth,
Than whan his name apalled is for age.
(3051-3053)

It would certainly not suit the Knight's style to say that his hero

... had a wife that held for contenance
A shop, and swyved for hir sustenance.
(4421-4422)

But only the word "honour" in the one passage and the word "swyved" in the other are stylistic clues in the narrower linguistic sense; and it is the choice of subject—the content—which prompts the choice of those words. The tellers choose their tales from the grab-bag of memory; the styles of all are a standard literary style, but we get such a vivid sense of their society and their individual lives, of subtle changes taking place in the social fabric, that content alone and a few touches of individual traits are enough to make us supply differing styles within this style—to make us believe or imagine that *le style c'est l'homme même.*

## THE IDEAL AND THE ACTUAL

To medieval men obsolescence, like all change, illustrated the mutability of the world and hence the vanity of human wishes. But Chaucer treated these standard medieval themes in a new way: he gave a vivid experience of temporality by drawing attention to the Prioress's golden keepsake, the Cook's warmed-over pies, the Merchant's regret, the Wife's nostalgia. He set these against a fragmented and largely forgotten past—the "old days," the days of the Bretons, the days when there were "fairie," when beasts and birds could talk and sing, when Phoebus dwelt here. And the "vivid" details are memorable but fleeting experiences—the Friar's sparkling eyes, the Pardoner's voice singing "the murierly and loude," the Miller's bagpipe that "brought us out of towne." Remembered time and recorded time are the stuff of narrative, and narrative creates a microcosmic eternity which outlasts the present day. We know that the Friar's name was Huberd and the Shipman's barge was called the Maudelayne, that the Host is named Harry Bailly and the Cook named Roger of Ware, not because their names were more important than anyone else's but because the poet snatched them, as if at random, from oblivion. But the random quality of these particularities puts us in mind of how much more has passed beyond our knowing.

This articulation of the passing of time is uniquely Chaucer's, but the picture it provides is a fundamental medieval conception, that of a world in decline from the "former age" or the Golden Age, growing old, becoming physically and morally weak. Chaucer gives explicit expression to this idea only once in *The Canterbury Tales*, in the ironic passage spoken by the Clerk at the end of his tale, which he had from Petrarch:

> This world is nat so strong, it is no nay,
> As it hath been in olde times yoore. . . .
> (1139-1140)

But the idea is implied in the General Prologue and throughout *The Canterbury Tales* by the pervasive sense of obsolescence. Chaucer shared this theme with Gower, who in the prologue of the *Confessio Amantis* announced his subject as the world which declines and renews itself daily:

> Thus I, which am a burel clerk
> Purpose for to write a book
> After the world that whilom took
> Long time in olde dayes passed:
> But for men sayn it is now lassed,
> In worse plit than it was tho,
> I thenke for to touch also
> The world which neweth every day. . . .
> (52-59)

Characteristically Chaucer shows in minute and accurate detail what "moral Gower" stated as a generality. But both poets agreed that the senescent world of medieval thought was not an emblem of despair. While the world is winding down from its first Golden Age, it also "neweth every day," and men can follow ideals of conduct which would impose upon the world a corrective and civilizing influence. It was not the Church alone which was to accomplish this but the state and the individual. So much the worse, then, if men and institutions flouted those ideals which might counter the world's decline.

The *Troilus* does not represent such a set of ideals in the past from which actualities have fallen off, and does not suggest that human effort can exert a corrective or civilizing influence; instead it shows a former civilization which did not have the advantage of Christian ideals. We see the men of this pre-Christian age groping blindly for ideals of conduct, worshipping false gods, caught up in an endless war whose purpose is all but forgotten. Their ideals are not forsaken but ill-formed. And the ideals singled out for scrutiny are identified with the chivalric and courtly ones which were the fashion of medieval aristocrats, valor and love. Troilus, the hero, is the idealist: his story is that of a failed, an inadequate ideal. From this point of view the *Troilus* is a critique of idealism itself. The great ideal of a love which ennobles is always immediate and before us, never a thing of the past, never tarnished. We see Troilus first cynical about love, then "converted." Pandarus cannot persuade him to reveal the reason for his sorrow until he happens upon that appeal which is to Troilus irresistible, the appeal to his idealism:

> What! many a man hath love full deer ybought
> Twenty winter that his lady wiste,
> That nevere yet his lady mouth he kiste.
>
> What! shold he therefore fallen in dispair,
> Or be recreant for his owne tene,
> Or sleen himself, al be his lady fair?
> Nay, nay, but ever in oon be fresh and greene
> To serve and love his deere hertes queene,
> And think it is a guerdon, hir to serve,
> A thousand fold more than he can deserve.
>                                    (I:810-819)

In these words Pandarus reminds Troilus of the noblest ideal of long-suffering love, and we learn at once "of that word took heede Troilus" (820). Troilus's high-mindedness is contrasted with the intelligent skepticism of Pandarus and the cautious pragmatism of Criseyde, but this is not such a violent contrast as some have thought. When Troilus in an unwonted moment of pragmatism suggests that the lovers steal away (IV:1503) Criseyde is able to present not only the practical reasons against such a move but the idealistic ones. She ends reminding Troilus just how high-minded a love they have and how important it is that this be maintained (1667-1687). Nor is Pandarus without ideals. He is steeped in the philosophy of the ancient world; we ought to understand that his wise saws and proverbs are part of his learning, the possession of one whose views have been formed by reading and thinking as much as—perhaps more than—by experience. And what Pandarus knows is true: times change, circumstances alter cases, everything has its time. It would be sensible for Troilus to follow his advice, forget Criseyde, eschew regret, start a new life. But it is just because of his idealism that he does not follow the pragmatic course which is the best Pandarus can recommend. The ideal which awed us at its poetical height turns into a false hope. We see this happen before our eyes. At the very end, when the narrator sadly draws his moral about "This world, that passeth soon as flowres faire," he implies that the audience still follows these hopeless "pagan" ideals and still needs to learn the lesson which the poem teaches. That lesson has never been more succinctly phrased than by Professor Donaldson: "The poem states, what much of Chaucer's poetry states, the necessity under which men lie of living in, making the best of, enjoying, and loving a world from which they must remain detached and which they must ultimately hate."

In *The Canterbury Tales* ideals are presented differently. If one could abstract from the *Troilus* that aspect which reveals love manqué, which views the ideal regretfully, which sees it far in the past and losing its luster, one would have the quality with which idealism is shown throughout *The Canterbury Tales*. But to abstract this would mean turning only to the ending, forgetting the immediacy and vibrancy with which ideals are treated throughout the poem. In *The Canterbury Tales* the narrative "now" focuses upon actualities and puts ideals back into the blur of history. The ideals which stand immediately before us are false and unappealing—the burghers' ambitions, the Pardoner's avarice, the class-conscious and money-grubbing motives which energize most of the pilgrims. The true ideals of the "ideal" pilgrims—the Knight's crusading spirit, the brotherhood of Parson and Plowman, perhaps the Clerk's selfless dedication—seem obsolescent. And the tales told by these ideal pilgrims do not reflect the luster which the ideal is presumed to have had in better days. In the Knight's tale an undercurrent of comic irony and a certain number of ridiculous circumstances or anticlimaxes undercut the romance idealism. The Clerk's tale ends with the Clerk's ironic admission that the ideal is no longer followed. And the Parson's tale, like the *Melibee*, represents not so much an ideal as the application of an ideal. The two prose treatises are practical, "how-to" works: the one tells members of the ruling class how to choose counselors, when to wage war, how to do justice, and so on; the other tells the Christian listener how to avoid sin and do penance. Both the prose works concentrate upon the effort men must make to carry out an ideal, not upon the ideal itself; and neither gives to its subject the luster and magnificence which the poetry of the *Troilus* gives to the ideal of love. The "ideal narratives" (like the Man of Law's, the Prioress's, or the Clerk's tales) are moral tales, but in the mouths of their tellers they become, as we shall see later, "misguided moralism"—moralism which fails to instruct the moralist himself. The single narrative which presents an ideal without discrediting it is the Second Nun's tale; but like all saints' legends it calls attention to ideals of perfection so high as to be reserved for those especially called, and so reminds us of our imperfection.

Ideals are false but lustrous in the *Troilus*, true but tarnished in *The Canterbury Tales*. So with actualities: in the *Troilus* they call for compromise with ideals, in *The Canterbury Tales* for new ideals or renewed ones. In the *Troilus* actuality is the everyday domestic life of the Trojan upper classes. We observe a style of life, customs and preoccupations wholly familiar to aristocrats of the fourteenth century—a day-to-day world of personal machinations, of polite conversations, of singing songs and reading aloud, attending religious ceremonies, following wars, worrying about love. It is a style of life for which medieval aristocrats themselves felt an enthusiasm and which the bourgeois took as a model. It is not a falling-off or decline from an imagined worthier past. What makes things go wrong, what decimates the idealized love, is the circumstantial or conditional actuality which accompanies every style of life. An exchange of prisoners is arranged, political decisions— wrong-headed ones—are arrived at in a parliament, and appropriate conduct dictates that the principals resign themselves to Criseyde's departure. In the background, blind chance, the goddess Fortune, presides over this circumstantial or conditional aspect of affairs. The pragmatism of everyday life calls for adjustment to altered cases. Criseyde among the Greeks must resign herself: it is unfeasible to return. Troilus must resign himself: she will not come back. And compromise is a condition of pragmatism—Troilus, outside the bedroom, must hold his tongue while he hears Pandarus lie, and the deception, without which the ideal would never come to fruition, tarnishes his conduct but not the ideal itself. There is a tension between ideals and those actualities of daily life which makes ideals impracticable.

In *The Canterbury Tales* there is no such tension. Ideals are in the past, actuality in the narrative "now." This is forced upon us in the General Prologue by the way the portraits end. The ideal portraits end with a sententia, a general statement: the Knight "was late ycome from his viage / And wente for to don his pilgrimage"; the Clerk would "gladly . . . lerne and gladly teche"; the Parson taught Christ's lore "but first he follwed it himselve." The other portraits end with a particular detail or a piquant phrase. The Squire carves before his father at the table, the Prioress wears her crowned A with its motto, the Wife knows of the "old dance," the Miller pipes the company out of town with a bagpipe, the Reeve rides at the rear of the procession, the Summoner bears with him a cake, the Pardoner sings merrily and loud. Names are sometimes used to end the portraits—the Friar is named Huberd, the Shipman's barge is the Maudelayne. The Franklin's portrait ends describing him with the obsolescent word "vavasour." Twice the narrator begs off, leaving details for us to surmise: he does not know the Merchant's name, will not say more of the Man of Law's array. He ends the portrait of the Guildsmen and their wives with the striking detail "a mantel royallich ybore," the portrait of the Manciple with the statement that he "set hir aller cappe." The portraits conclude by encapsulating the pilgrim, making him vivid and memorable. These details suggest an inner reality, the reality of each pilgrim's character, frame of mind, place in society—the very realities which will dictate their choice and treatment of tales.

The *Troilus*, then, gives us a picture of an ordered social unit in a society which existed before the age of grace and is about to be swallowed up in the process of history; we know where it is headed. *The Canterbury Tales* gives us a picture of a disordered Christian society in a state of obsolescence, decline, and uncertainty; we do not know where it is headed. The *Troilus* shows us noble if inadequate ideals and a glittery actuality whose fate is sealed; *The Canterbury Tales* shows us ideals no longer followed and an evanescent actuality whose fate is unknown. Both works teach contempt of the world, but the *Troilus* teaches that lesson by fastening chiefly upon the themes of mutability and vanity. *The Canterbury Tales* fastens upon the other themes of *contemptus mundi* writings—upon the corruptness of human nature and society and the world's decline. Both works are ambivalent about the vanity of human wishes, pursuits, and efforts; so were the treatises on contempt of the world. Pope Innocent III in his classic treatise (which Chaucer says he translated) inveighed against the vanity of curiosity and learning, but when he fastened upon actualities—the corrupt judge, the avaricious lawyer, the lecherous priest—he implied that reform was needed. That is the seed of satire, perhaps the real origin of medieval satire: Bernard of Morval actually called his *De contemptu mundi* a satire. And the implication that things should be reformed is present in *The Canterbury Tales*—present in the minute actualities of its un-ideal characters and present in the author's irony. The great ideas of the Middle Ages—the mutability, vanity, and corruption of the world, the decline of the world from a Golden Age, the need of the individual to transcend in his thoughts the mundane order, the need for charity and reform—all get into *The Canterbury Tales*. But it is not enough to find them spread here and there in explicit statements or suggested in emblems and allegories. They are there in actualities, in the way events and people are presented—or, I should have said, in the way we are made to see them.

CHARLES A. OWEN, JR.

# The Importance of the Literal

The *Canterbury Tales* is a collection of stories. It is also a narrative of some thirty people journeying from Southwark to Canterbury and back. As the first, it reflects a medieval literary convention. As the second, it absorbs the first, suggesting in its imperfections, its contradictions and inconsistencies, the experimental nature of Chaucer's art. As Chaucer worked on the fiction of the pilgrimage, the received meanings of such a fiction gave place to the developing significance of the interacting elements. The stories tended to become expressive of character. Often overtly didactic, they tested themselves against each other and against the increasingly stated and hence objectified purposes of the narrators. From the conflicts and contrasts and consonances, and from the complex relationships thus set up, emerged a series of patterns, which the reader both enjoys and perceives as significant. Though these patterns are only implicitly meaningful, they often contrast with the overt didacticism of the narrators; they come to serve as the standard against which the visions of all the narrators are measured; they constitute a level of value independent of any one story or any narrator; they give the reader a purely aesthetic enjoyment—the kind a creator might have who watches the independent actions of his own creatures. The "game" of the storytelling replaces the "ernest" of overt morality as the source of value. The "game" of holiday travel yields richer meaning than the "ernest" of pilgrimage. Hence the paradox of a "game" more "ernest" than "ernest," of value enjoyed as pattern.

Two things especially contribute to the dynamics of emergent pattern in the *Canterbury Tales*. They appear as two sides of the same coin in the passage where Chaucer first apologizes for some of the words he will have to report:

From *The Pilgrimage and Storytelling in The Canterbury Tales*. Copyright © 1977 by University of Oklahoma Press.

> Whoso shal telle a tale after a man,
> He moot reherce as ny as evere he kan
> Everich a word. . . .
>
> (A 733)

Here, in disclaiming his own responsibility for what the pilgrims say, he is giving them an autonomy, a freedom from authorial control; he is pointing to their characters as the source of initiative; he is providing the base for the major interactions in the narrative of journey, the relationship of character to tale and the relationship of characters and of tales with each other. He is also proclaiming the most drastic slice-of-life naturalism in the annals of literature. "Everich a word" does not even permit a slicing of reality. The whole pilgrimage will be there—no untruth, no feigning things, no paraphrase. The autonomy of all agents and the literal accuracy of the report—these two ingredients condition what happens in the *Canterbury Tales*. The fiction is that there is no fiction. The result, as in Dante, is a polysemous narrative and an affirmation of beneficent rule by the "sighte above," but in naturalistic rather than supernatural terms. Chaucer fixes his attention on the Canterbury Way, on the words and actions and visions of his pilgrims.

One set of references is especially impressive, not only as showing his intimate knowledge of the whole Canterbury road and his intention to use the road as an element in a meaningful pattern, but also as implying the structural import of the stages of the journey. In the G fragment, as the pilgrims near Canterbury, they are overtaken by a canon and his yeoman at a small village called Boughton, in the Blee Forest. Chaucer not only knows the name of this hamlet but also knows its exact position—the halfway point of the short journey from Ospring to Canterbury—and this detail makes it clear that the day's journey began at Ospring, though he does not mention that town by name:

> Sires, now in the morwe-tyde
> Out of youre hostelrie I saugh yow ryde.
>
> (G 589)

Chaucer makes of Boughton a significant turning point. The pilgrims have been listening to the Second Nun's rendering of the life of St. Cecilia, but they are distracted from the religious commitment appropriate to the day they reach their pilgrimage's goal—distracted by the drama of the Yeoman's conversion and the Canon's flight, and by the Yeoman's account of alchemy as honest but futile experiment on the one hand, and as villainous but effective skullduggery on the other. The base metals are not transformed into gold by the efforts of either of the two canons, nor by proximity to the great martyr's shrine. The Yeoman boasts, before his conversion, of his master's skill:

That al this ground on which we been ridyng,
Til that we come to Caunterbury toun,
He koude al clene turne it up-so-doun,
And pave it al of silver and of gold.

(G 626)

The boast is vain; the road remains a road. But the events add level on level of
meaning to the literal—the Canon's flight from exposure to the community
of pilgrims; the Yeoman's pride in what blowing an alchemist's fire for seven
years has taught him; his foolish moral fervor against the tricky Canon's con
game; the cost in quality of life of the effort to extract wealth from matter; and
the contrasting stories on what was probably the middle day of a five-day
pilgrimage, a day that began at an inn in Ospring and ended, no doubt, at
another inn in Canterbury, a day that included the visit to the shrine of St.
Thomas. Far from superseding the literal, the values depend on "everich a
word." Chaucer sought increasingly through his art the effect of real pilgrims
on a real road, their overnight stops the inevitable punctuation of their
storytelling activity.

Through their efforts to create, through their quarrels and discussions
and confessions, we see not only their intentions, their conscious image of
themselves, but also on occasion the inadvertent self-revelation that gives
depth to the character. These occasions constitute the great moments of the
pilgrimage. The Prioress, the Nun's Priest, the Wife of Bath, the Pardoner,
and the Merchant stamp themselves vividly on our consciousness. That
others make a less telling impact does not disturb the potential. At any
moment the quarrel may flare up that exposes a Reeve, a Friar, or a Summoner. The Franklin is moved by more generous sentiments to involve
himself in the "game," while Chaucer and the Clerk wait patiently to be
noticed and pilgrims like the Monk, the Physician, the Second Nun, and the
Man of Law seek an anonymity in the stereotypes of genre. The range of
vividness from Wife of Bath to Second Nun suggests a planned maximum, but
the steps in between are plausibly haphazard. The relationships thus set up
between the meaning of the tale, the purpose of the narrator, and his
inadvertent self-revelation, compounded as the tales proceed by every con-
ceivable type of cross-reference, create the sense of meaningful pattern that
constitutes the equivalent of the anagoge in medieval allegory. The reading
of meanings on this level, dependent still on accurate attention to "everich a
word," is primarily an aesthetic experience. The naive expression of a
mimetic aim by the narrator reflects Chaucer's confidence, to be sensed
everywhere in the *Canterbury Tales*, that faithful imitation yields the truest
values.

Chaucer's escape from the shackles of medieval didacticism is, as one
would expect, not absolute. At some point after he started the *Canterbury*

*Tales*, he was moved to retract his greatest work as a poet. Whether he recovered from this excessive religiosity or ended in it will never be certainly known. What has given his work its humane appeal over the ages is its singular freedom from the excesses associated with *Zeitgeist*. Once its terms are understood and its language mastered, Chaucer's work speaks to us in a timeless idiom with an artistry we need no key to unlock. It can perhaps be seen as an expression of our own *Zeitgeist* that, having contributed so much to the dissemination of Chaucer's poetry, we have tended of late to emphasize its narrowly medieval elements, to derive from it a series of specialized and esoteric meanings, to force it to conform to a thesis-ridden vision. To the extent that we have done so, we have broken with the classical line of critics extending from Dryden through Blake and Coleridge to Kittredge and Lowes and Muscatine. Their emphasis on his richly peopled world and on the skill of the art that projects it, on what Dryden called "God's plenty," reaches back to what one of the first men to read the *Canterbury Tales* saw in it. When ordering illuminations for the several tales, the Ellesmere editor had the artists illustrate each tale, not with a scene from the story itself, but with the portrait of the pilgrim telling it.

The problem that the Ellesmere editor and the men responsible for the other early manuscript arrangements tried to conceal makes the *Canterbury Tales* unique among the great literary works of our civilization. Its incompleteness, especially its fragmentary incompleteness, presents a challenge few recent editors have chosen to face. What we have represents at least three different plans for the whole work—an early beginning for the storytelling marked, among other things, by the Wife of Bath telling the *Shipman's Tale*, a later arrangement with the Wife detached from the opening sequence and telling her own tale, and another arrangement in which the number of tales each pilgrim is to tell has been changed from one to four or from four to one. The plausible expedient is to accept one of the early arrangements, ignoring as insoluble the related problems of the proper tale order, the days of the journey, and the development of Chaucer's conception of his work.

Support for this expedient is derived from the extreme unlikelihood that thirty people on horseback could hear one another telling stories on a narrow medieval road. The basic fiction being so totally unrealistic, no notice need be taken of the place names scattered here and there to give an aura of authenticity. Chaucer apparently took some cognizance of this objection himself. A number of times he has the Host call people to him when he chooses them for the next tale. Thus the Host says to Chaucer:

> Approche neer, and looke up murily.
> Now war yow, sires, and lat this man have place!
> (B 1889)

Similarly, in turning from the Monk to the Nun's Priest, he says, "Com neer, thou preest, com hyder, thou sir John!" (B 4000). And in the Manciple's Prologue, when he spots the Cook riding behind in a drunken stupor, he not only tries to have him wakened but summons him:

> Do hym come forth, he knoweth his penaunce;
> For he shall telle a tale, by my fey.
>
> (H 13)

In the Canon's Yeoman's Prologue the Canon draws near the group at the center to overhear what his Yeoman is telling the Host (G 684 ff.). Had he been aware of the line the Host's questioning was taking, he would surely have intervened sooner and perhaps avoided the necessity for flight. The impression Chaucer gives is of the Host riding in the midst of the group, the current storyteller near him, and some pilgrims—like the Cook when he is sleeping off a night's debauch—not listening.

In any event, the citing of one improbability does not really justify ignoring the evidence provided by the realistic references to places on the road and to the time of day, especially when, combined with a recognition of development, they provide some explanation for the fragments in which Chaucer left his work. Turning our backs on these interrelated problems ends any effort to understand how the *Canterbury Tales* came to be what it is. The experience of a work in progress, its form emerging from the interaction of the parts in the imagination of the author, underlies and rewards an accurate reading of a work less than a quarter finished.

Strangely enough, the strongest element in the interacting parts that absorbed the creative energies of Chaucer's last years is not the powerful medieval motif of pilgrimage. Once the Host has made a community of the group at his inn, the pilgrims become storytellers. The climax of their activities becomes in the final plan the prize-awarding supper at the Tabard. In a sense, the storytelling contest supplants the pilgrimage. Of course nothing prevents those so inclined from directing their storytelling to the same end as the pilgrimage. Few of the pilgrims in fact choose this option. The Pardoner even mocks it with his cynical performance. Recognition of this opposition between art and religion perhaps motivates in part the Parson's outburst against the Host's swearing. The successful diversion of most of his fellows from the religious concern motivating their decision to go on pilgrimage and their immersion in the "game" proposed by the Host must have irked the Parson beyond silent endurance. That the Host easily turns aside the attack and is not again challenged until, at the end, he must call on the Parson for a tale, speaks more for the enthusiasm the idea of storytelling has aroused in the pilgrims than for any special capacities Harrie Baillie has for his self-imposed duties. In any other context the Host would be no match for the Parson. The same is true of all the associated oppositions created in the work: Canterbury versus Southwark, the Cathedral versus the Tabard, the consecrated wafer and wine paid for in the crucifixion versus the "soper at oure aller cost." The disparities are ludicrous. Yet the "game" dominates. It creates the meanings and values that absorb our attention and compel our imagination. The literal reality of a road, of men and women, of the story-telling and the comment it occasions, of, finally, an organized game, a contest, imitates successfully the complex interrelationships of a society; it generates experienced values that transcend the society and even rational definition. The Host can smugly tell the victims of his crude banter not to be "wroth": "A man may seye ful sooth in game and pley" (A 4355). Or again: "Ful ofte in game a sooth I have herd seye!" (B 3154). One of his victims replies, "But 'sooth pley, quaad pley,' as the Flemyng seith" (A 4357). And Chaucer himself says, "And eek man shal nat maken earnest of game" (A 3186).

SAUL NATHANIEL BRODY

# Truth and Fiction in the "Nun's Priest's Tale"

Readers of the *Nun's Priest's Tale* must be struck by the simplicity of the plot. A rooster in a barnyard has what he takes to be a prophetic dream in which a hound-like beast enters the yard. One of his hens hears him groaning, and after she wakens him, they engage in a debate over whether or not the dream is a forecast of things to come. However, in spite of his own argument that the dream is prophetic, the rooster is so taken with the hen's beauty that he disregards the dream's warning altogether. Thus, upon entering the barnyard, the fox is easily able to flatter and seize the rooster. Nevertheless, through an appeal to the fox's pride, the rooster outsmarts and escapes from him.

All this is narrated in an unhurried, considered fashion. Everything is detailed and made plain. There is room and time to introduce the dairy-woman who owns the rooster; to describe Chaunticleer's colors; to allow the chickens to argue at length about dreams in direct discourse; to describe the tumult on the farm as the fox is pursued. The fanciful life of the barnyard comes alive through elaborate description and faithfully rendered conversation, so that finally everything seems exact—not merely the setting, but even the colors of the animals and their feelings.

The story is so simple, and it is told with such precision, that the narrator could almost be taken to have witnessed the events he describes. Were it not that the tale is about speaking chickens in a barnyard, we might be tempted to call it realistic. But of course an obvious fact about the tale is that although the Nun's Priest presents it as something true and reasonable, he also makes it whimsical, extravagant, and unrealistic. His tale is thus

From *The Chaucer Review* 14, no. 1. Copyright © 1979 by The Pennsylvania State University Press.

paradoxically both absurd and serious, realistic and unrealistic, fictive and true, and that paradox, that tension between the literature-like and the life-like, is central to the tale. It is the source at once of much of its humor and much of its point, for through it the Nun's Priest asserts the ultimate seriousness not simply of his fiction, but of all fiction.

The passage that opens the tale, in which the Nun's Priest introduces the widow and her farm and chickens, is shaped to emphasize the linking of fiction and truth in the narrative. The description of the old woman stresses her reality, the conditions of her life. In a few lines (4011-36), we learn about her advanced age; her cottage (narwe and sooty); her three sows and three cows; her one sheep, named Malle; her diet; the fact that as a consequence she suffers from neither gout nor apoplexy; and her patient acceptance of her humble life. In all this, the Nun's Priest may be offering implicit comment on such women as the Prioress and the Wife of Bath, but he is also preparing us for the chickens, who are more the subject of the story than the widow who owns them. In fact, it is precisely through the contrast between the chickens and their owner that the narrator reminds us that he is telling a tale and we are listening to it.

The introductory description of Chaunticleer and Pertelote begins with the same objective concentration on reality that marks the introduction of the widow:

> A yeerd she hadde, enclosed al aboute
> With stikkes, and a drye dych withoute,
> In which she hadde a cok, hight Chauntecleer.
> (4037-39)

But by the end of the passage, the teller has left the widow's prosaic world far behind, and entered into the poetic realm of a splendid rooster who not only can tell time perfectly, but who also is surrounded by a courtly harem of hens, among whom is his favorite, *damoysele Pertelote*; and they sing *In sweete accord, "My lief is faren in londe!"* (4040-69). The Nun's Priest's performance is magnificent, capable, I think, of seducing some of us into accepting the absurd reality of the chickens, or at least of not critically questioning it. And the narrator makes it seem as if that is exactly what he wants. At just the point where he tells us that his chickens sing lyrics, he interrupts his narrative to point out that it is not fictive, but historically reliable: "For thilke tyme, as I have understonde, / Beestes and briddes koude speke and synge" (4070-71). Of course, his actual (if implicit) assertion is that we are hearing a story, not objective truth, and naturally that assertion is exactly the one the narrator wants us to catch.

The Nun's Priest's device is traditional and simple. By dissolving dramatic illusion, he forces us to a heightened awareness of the tale as a work of fiction, as art and not reality itself. Significantly, each time he interrupts himself, he does the same thing, and he does it often enough and in such a way as to suggest that he is asking the audience to consider the implications not only of his storytelling, but also of storytelling itself.

Having suspended the action at lines 4070-71, he picks it up in the next line, *And so bifel that in a dawenynge*, and continues without interruption until line 4373. The scene centers on the discussion between Chaunticleer and Pertelote of Chaunticleer's prophetic dream, Pertelote urging him to put no stock in it and the rooster defending the value of such dreams by offering *exempla* that illustrate how prophetic dreams come true. It is important to note that Chaunticleer, engaged in an interpretative act, uses stories to illustrate a truth, and, what is just as important, he pays no attention to the point of his *exempla*. At the end of his speech, immediately after determining that *I shal han of this avisioun / Adversitee* (4342-43), he draws such joy from the presence of Pertelote that he puts all thought of disaster from his mind. In one way, all this can be taken as a comment on the Monk's use of *exempla*, but in another and related way it clearly raises the larger question of the relation of stories to moral truth and human behavior.

The Nun's Priest draws our attention to this larger matter by once again interrupting his narrative, this time at exactly the point where Chaunticleer is ignoring the import of his own *exempla*. The digression begins with a clear break in the storytelling:

> Thus roial, as a prince is in his halle,
> Leve I this Chauntecleer in his pasture,
> And after wol I telle his aventure.
> (4374-76)

It ends with an equally clear return to the story: "Now wol I torne agayn to my sentence" (4404). By breaking into the fictional world and suspending its progress, the digression emphasizes that a story is being told, much as does an intermission in a theater. Here, as the curtain falls, Chaunticleer is compared to a prince; in what follows, the Nun's Priest tells us how on a particular day Chaunticleer identified the date and felt *revel and solas* in his heart. In this passage, a section that begins a lengthy digression, the Nun's Priest prepares us for what is to follow by giving his chickens human qualities, something he does in fact throughout the tale, presumably not only for comic effect, for the sake of absurdity, but also to keep us aware of the story's implications for human beings.

Consider the number of times and ways the Nun's Priest explicitly establishes parallels between chickens and people. In his first aside, he explains that at the time of Chaunticleer, beasts and birds could speak and sing. Later, while dreaming, Chaunticleer groans like a man vexed (4078). Pertelote challenges him by demanding whether, having a beard, he also has the heart of a man (4110). Chaunticleer later says that he would give his shirt to have Pertelote read the legend of Kenelm (4310-11), and later still the Nun's Priest quotes Chaunticleer's remarks on the baneful advice of women—women, not hens (4446-56). He compares Chaunticleer's terror to a man's (4467-68). The fox tells the rooster that he never heard a man sing as Chaunticleer's father did (4491-92), and when Chaunticleer tries to outsing his father, he spreads his wings like a man who could not see his betrayal (4512-13). And as Pertelote is compared to Hasdrubal's wife (4452-53), so are the other hens compared to epic women (4545-51, 4559-63). Whatever else these passages may do, they all serve the same purpose as the Nun's Priest's interruptions of his story, that is, they compel us to take a critical view of it, to focus on the story's implications for human beings. And the result is that by absurdly comparing chickens to people, the Nun's Priest keeps us from holding illusions about either. Chaunticleer may be as royal as a prince, but he is in his yard, every moment the cock, and every moment the embodiment of foolish masculine pride and arrogance.

In the same way, and for the same reason, starting at line 4377, the Nun's Priest has us think of Chaunticleer as both chicken and man. When March (*whan God first maked man*), April and more than two days of May had gone by, Chaunticleer, accompanied by his *sevene wyves*, calculated that it was prime. He did this, we are told, by observing that the sun had climbed forty-one degrees and then some. Apart from the other implications of the narrator's and Chaunticleer's attention to date and time, one sure effect of the entire passage is the humanizing of Chaunticleer, who makes a very human calculation on a day in the human calendar while surrounded by his wives. And the narrator's remark that Chaunticleer could make such calculations *by kynde, and by noon oother loore* (4386; compare 4505) only serves to heighten our perception of the rooster as a man/cock, just as does his earlier comment that in Chaunticleer's time birds and beasts could sing words.

It is through this humanizing, through the comment that Chaunticleer went out walking *in al his pryde* (4381), and through Chaunticleer's remark that his heart is full of *revel and solas* (4393) that the narrator sets us up for his prediction of the coming disaster and his observation on the transcience of worldly joy. The language echoes the Monk's earlier remarks on the nature of tragedy, the catastrophes that befall men, and the Nun's Priest emphasizes the truth of the axiom that *worldly joye is soone ago* (4396) by suggesting that if a rhetorician knew how, he might enter it in a chronicle, *As for a sovereyn notabilitee* (4399). Thus, by interrupting the narrative, the Nun's Priest reminds us that it is a work of fiction about a laughable cock who perhaps ought in one light to be taken seriously, for the bird is about to experience a virtually human catastrophe in a virtually human way.

The audience, continues the priest, should understand that the story is a true story—as true, that is, as the story of Lancelot:

> Now every wys man, lat him herkne me;
> This storie is also trewe, I undertake,
> As is the book of Launcelot de Lake,
> That wommen holde in ful greet reverence.
> (4400-03)

The reference to Lancelot here is curious, and commentators have not been able to make much sense of it. While it now seems to be generally agreed that the Nun's Priest is referring to the version of the Lancelot story mentioned in Dante's *Inferno*, Canto V, "the famous romance Paolo and Francesca were reading when their love dawned," there is little accord over the significance of the allusion. For example, it has been taken as pointless, "except as an ironical aside" (Baugh), or as an assertion by the Nun's Priest that his story is not a true story at all, or as "possibly a comic allusion to the tragic consequences of Francesca's interest in the *matière de Bretagne*." The reference, however, is neither pointless, nor simply a way of underlining the fictional nature of the story, nor merely a comic suggestion of Francesca's fate. On the contrary, it is very much to the point, not least of all because it emphasizes the interplay between truth and fiction in the *Nun's Priest's Tale*.

In Canto V of the *Inferno*, Dante asks Francesca how it was that she and Paolo came to know they were in love:

> Ma dimmi: "al tempo d'i dolci sospiri,
> a che e come concedette amore
> che conosceste i dubbiosi disiri?".
>     E quella a me: "Nessun maggior dolore
> che ricordarsi del tempo felice
> ne la miseria; e ciò sa 'l tuo dottore.
>     Ma s'a conoscer la prima radice
> del nostro amor tu hai cotanto affetto,
> dirò come colui che piange e dice.
>     Noi leggiavamo un giorno per diletto
> di Lancialotto come amor lo strinse;
> soli eravamo e sanza alcun sospetto.
>     Per più fiate li occhi ci sospinse
> quella lettura, e scolorocci il viso;
> ma solo un punto fu quel che ci vinse.
>     Quando leggemmo il disiato riso
> esser basciato da cotanto amante,
> questi, che mai da me non fia diviso,
>     la bocca mi basciò tutto tremante.
> Galeotto fu 'l libro e chi lo scrisse:
> quel giorno più non vi leggemmo avante".

Though the certainty of it seems to have escaped commentators on the
allusion in the *Nun's Priest's Tale*, Chaucer knew the passage in Dante, and
knew it well—well enough to select the first three lines of Francesca's speech
for Pandarus in *Troilus and Criseyde*:

> For of fortunes sharpe adversitee
> The worste kynde of infortune is this,
> A man to han ben in properitee,
> And it remembren, whan it passed is.
> (III, 1625-28)

But why does he have the Nun's Priest refer to the Paolo and Francesca
episode? An examination of it suggests three reasons.

First, Francesca's reversal of fortune, emphasized in lines 121-23 of
Canto V, is matched by Chaunticleer's own reversal. Note the juxtaposition
between Chaunticleer's line, "Ful is myn herte of revel and solas!" (4393),
and the Nun's Priest's comment immediately following, which emphasizes
that he thinks of Chaunticleer's downfall in terms of shifting *felicitas*, or
*welfulness*:

> But sodeynly hym fil a sorweful cas,
> For evere the latter ende of joye is wo.
> (4934-95)

Second, both Francesca and Chaunticleer suffer for similar reasons: in
each case, seized by sexual desire, the lovers surrender reason, and with
disastrous results.

Third, the story that Francesca tells of the first root of her and Paolo's
love itself makes a point relevant to the Nun's Priest's purposes, namely, that
there is an intimate relationship between stories about human behavior and
human behavior itself. Francesca describes how she and Paolo were reading
about Lancelot in *Galeotto*, and how—when they read of the kiss that
Lancelot gave to Guinevere—they themselves kissed, and that day read no
more. The role of *Galeotto* as a pandar calls notice to the particular moral
sense in which the Nun's Priest, perhaps with some irony, considers his tale to
be as true as the Lancelot story: not only in that it represents a typical human
action, the succumbing to sexual passion, but also in that as a story it is
capable of influencing human behavior.

Hence, the Nun's Priest's entire digression in lines 4374-4404 can be
seen to be a calculated and unified piece. In its first section (4374-94),
Chaunticleer is likened to a man approaching the latter end of joy. He is
almost human in his ability to tell time, but though he may be excellent at it,
he fails to realize either that the day (May 3) is a *dies malus*, a day of ill luck, or
that his own reasoning regarding prophetic dreams should keep him on guard.
Instead, he looks into Pertelote's scarlet-red eyes, fear leaves him, and sexual

desire takes over. True *cok* that he is, he feathers and treads Pertelote forty times before prime, helping to produce the *revel and solas* that he feels at prime. In the second part of the digression (4395-99), in a transition, the priest comments on the transcience of worldly joy and looks ahead to the coming disaster. And in the last section (4400-04), he suggests that his tale has real implications, for Chaunticleer, the cock who is so like a human person, surrenders his reason in the way men and women do, as stories should remind us. The downfall of Chaunticleer is as true as the story of the downfall of Lancelot, which itself produced the story of the downfall of Paolo and Francesca. As a whole, then, the digression emphasizes that while the tale of Chaunticleer is only about a mere comical rooster, it nonetheless holds a mirror up to human behavior.

It is significant that the major asides by the Nun's Priest which follow in the narrative are devoted to producing the same understanding as does this first long digression. At line 4404, he announces that he is beginning his story again, and in the next eleven lines he describes how the fox breaks into the yard and waits for his chance to capture Chaunticleer, as murderers of men do. The mention of *homycides* (4414) leads to another extended digression, this one of forty lines (4416-56). It begins with the comparison of the fox to the three greatest traitors in history; goes on to apostrophize Chaunticleer for not following the warning in his dream; raises and then drops the question of whether Chaunticleer had any choice in the matter; and blames women for their bad advice, with the priest citing Chaunticleer as the source of such an attack—he himself, he says, *kan noon harm of no womman divyne* (4456). As before, the Nun's Priest consciously stimulates in us the dual perception of the animals as having and not having human qualities: the fox is a new Judas, a new Ganelon, and a new Sinon; and Chaunticleer follows the advice of his wife, who like all women, and another woman in particular (Eve), gives bad advice. But the fox hides in a bed of herbs, and all the discussion of whether or not Chaunticleer had free will is irrelevant to beasts: "I wol nat han to do of swich mateere; / My tale is of a cok, as ye may heere" . . . (4441-42). The priest, remembering that his story is about animals, stops himself from raising problems pertinent only to people. He may seem to be saying that his tale contains no lessons for humanity, that it is merely a tale and ought not to be taken seriously, but as before he also emphasizes that if the story is only *of a cok*, it is surely filled with reminders of how human beings do themselves in.

So too in his next asides. Having described how Chaunticleer was overcome by flattery, he turns to the lords in his audience and warns them against flatterers in their courts (4515-20). What happens to Chaunticleer in a barnyard contains warnings for England. Seven lines later, having described the capture of the rooster, the Nun's Priest stops the action again (4528-64), this time to offer a series of rhetorically inflated apostrophes (to destiny,

Venus, and Geoffey of Vinsauf), complaints, and comparisons (of the hens to lamenting women). Though Chaunticleer is only a rooster, he is subject to destiny, serves the goddess of love, and deserves to be written about in elaborate terms—as if he were a man, as if what happens to him were important to men.

There are thus three major digressions in the tale, and they all point to the presence of truth in the Nun's Priest's fiction. The first ends with the suggestion that stories, including the Nun's Priest's own, can mirror human passions accurately and thereby influence human behavior, or at least perceptions of the human condition; the second indicates that even a comic story about animals can echo human catastrophes and raise the sorts of questions that human catastrophes do, questions about the influences of women and predestination, for example; and the third digression, with its string of comically deflating mock-heroic passages, once again implicitly brings forward the parallel between the tale's animal world and the world of men. Taken together, then, the narrator's digressions and asides carefully pave the way for his closing reminder that although the tale may be a *folye*, it contains truth:

> But ye that holden this tale a folye,
> As of a fox, or of a cok and hen,
> Taketh the moralite, goode men.
> (4628-30)

Of course, exactly what the *moralite* is has never been generally agreed upon. Some find it among the moral statements that end the narrative: Chaunticleer's warning against blindness to flattery (4619-22), the fox's against speaking when it is better to be quiet (4623-25), and the narrator's against heedlessness, negligence, and flattery (4626-27). Others find it in various lessons implicit in the text, such as warnings against lechery or against human failings revealed through allegorical interpretation. And still others, recognizing the comic bent of the tale and finding a precise moral absent, caution against taking the tale too seriously, or pinpointing its lesson too precisely, or finding a lesson at all. Indeed, in the face of the varied lessons that have been discovered on and beneath the surface of the Nun's Priest's narrative—and rejected, a safe course would appear to be to avoid defining *the* lesson at all. On the other hand, the very presence of besetting ambiguity in the tale may indicate that if the work does contain a moral, that moral has to do with ambiguity itself—and most particularly with the ambiguity surrounding what is true and not true in the tale.

This final, central focus on the ambiguous intent of the *Nun's Priest's Tale* is anticipated in part by smaller ambiguities of language and intent within the tale. Three examples come readily to mind.

One is the reference to *the book of Launcelot de Lake, / That wommen holde in ful greet reverence* (4402-03). These lines can be translated in two ways: "the book of Lancelot, who held women in great esteem," and "the book of Lancelot, that women hold in great esteem." Taken the first way, the lines point to Lancelot's destructive sexuality, and by extension to the unreasonable passion of Chaunticleer and males like him, while the second translation implies a comment on the female response either to such males or to books about them—with the implicit warning that women, and perhaps the Prioress herself, ought not to repeat Francesca's error in surrendering to passion. The ambiguity is thoroughly functional, emphasizing as it does the question of whether it is male or female carnality that is to blame for the problems that beset humanity.

The second example is the well-known Latin translation by Chaunticleer:

> For al so siker as *In principio,*
> *Mulier est hominis confusio,*—
> Madame, the sentence of this Latyn is,
> "Womman is mannes joye and al his blis."
> (4353-56)

Here, of course, the question is whether Chaunticleer's mistranslation should be taken as intentional or not, or, to put it another way, whether Chaunticleer is conscious of the threat women pose and, even further, of the threat his own carnality poses. As in the previous example, the ambiguity calls attention to whether blame should be placed on the male, or the female, or both.

The third instance is the narrator's comment on the related statement that

> Wommennes conseils been ful oft colde;
> Wommannes conseil broghte us first to wo,
> And made Adam fro Paradys to go,
> Ther as he was ful myrie and wel at ese.
> (4446-49)

"These are the cock's words, and not mine," he says, *I kan noon harm of no womman divyne* (4456), meaning that he can not speak any harm about any woman, or (possibly referring to the Prioress, who could be expected to be offended by his remarks), that he knows nothing harmful about any divine woman. In this case, the ambiguity is whether the narrator wishes to be understood as not condemning women generally or just secular women, whether he is speaking of the condition of all men or just of himself, and finally whether he holds the Prioress, himself, or them both answerable for his own situation. Once again, the issue is male-female responsibility.

Chaunticleer is, no doubt, the embodiment not simply of that problem but also of the larger uncertainty in the tale over what is true and not true
generally. Though a rooster who scratches for corn, he is nevertheless capable
of speaking, and what is more, of speaking truth, the truth about dreams, a
truth he demonstrates by recourse to stories. A fantastical talking rooster, he
appears in the middle of a piece of fiction that poses as truth, tells a series of
*exempla* drawn largely (though not entirely) from authoritative sources, and
then ignores the truth contained in them. The consequence is that he suffers
a reversal of fortune, leading the narrator to remark that the story is as true as
the story of Lancelot, itself an acknowledged piece of fiction. Like his story,
Chaunticleer himself has a dual nature. He is true and fictive, rational and
irrational, magnificent and trivial, human and animal.

Accordingly, when he moralizes on what has happened to him, he
draws a lesson that is not so straightforwardly moral as it seems. Chaunticleer
warns against being blind, presumably to flattery, but it is only by using
flattery that he manages to escape from the fox; hence, while he does seem to
have come to a realization about the danger of pride, he has been able to
survive only by appealing to pride in someone else. Moreover, the lessons
drawn by the fox and the narrator are similarly ambiguous. Although the fox
warns against speaking foolishly, one can only suppose that if he again had
the opportunity to capture and eat Chaunticleer, he would do so. And while
the narrator's warning against heedlessness and flattery is morally sound from
one point of view, from another and more cynical one it can be taken as a
recommendation to villains (such as the fox) to keep their own interests
firmly in view. In brief, all the lessons drawn at the close of the story are
ambiguous, and for the very good reason that the human heart is ambiguous.

What then is the point of the *Nun's Priest's Tale?* I take it that the
story is about the complexity of things, about the elusiveness of truth and the
need to pursue it. It does not really matter whether Chaunticleer's downfall is
brought about by his lechery, his wife's advice, his susceptibility to flattery,
his recklessness, or unknowable influences such as destiny. The heart of the
matter is that Chaunticleer has a rational side that could have protected him,
and he ought to have known better than to ignore it. At the end, perched in
the tree, he sees that his survival will depend on his alertness in the future, his
use of his higher faculties. Of course, his lower, his animal impulses, will
always be ready to do him in, and that is his problem, as (the Nun's Priest
would say) it is everyone's problem.

In short, one apparent truth about the tale is that it will not easily
support one meaning, and if it is confused and ambiguous, if its moral is
elusive, if it can be seen from a variety of angles, that is because the tale is less
about a particular moral in it than about the very existence of moral possibilities. Accordingly, I suggest that the tale's lesson, its *fruyt*, is not to avoid,

say, flattery, but to recognize that difficult moral choices are everywhere. The narrator, in raising all sorts of possibilities of meaning, compels the audience to confront the ambiguities raised in the tale, and he thus creates in his fiction a mirror of what individuals regularly confront in life. What moral meaning they extract from or impose upon life, or the story, presumably depends upon their ethical predispositions, and their burden is to make the right choices.

In other words, the tale echoes experience, as all stories do, and echoes it convincingly by presenting elusive truths. The story itself is offered as both true and untrue, Chaunticleer is said both to be and not to be responsible for what happens to him, and the morals drawn at the end are both edifying and reconcilable with principles of pure self-interest. In the special sense in which the point of the poem is to be found in its confusion, the remark that its *fruyt* is its *chaf* is highly pertinent, as is the observation that the work's "shifting of focus . . . itself virtually constitutes the theme." For all these reasons, to appropriate one more critic's words, "the narrator cannot offer a guarantee that he has a moral by which he has shaped it; he can only offer St. Paul's guarantee that everything that has been written has a moral in it somewhere." Therefore, just as Chaunticleer must try to find meaning in what happens to him, so must the reader try to find meaning in what he reads.

The Nun's Priest is saying that any story—*al that writen is* (4631)—can be seen to have moral implications, not only stories told by a monk, but even an absurd piece of fiction by a priest about a cock, or an *exemplum* offered by that cock within the tale. To sharpen our perception of his own tale, he makes it altogether impossible to suspend disbelief. He frequently and consciously calls attention to himself as a story teller and to the poem as a story. *I telle yow my tale* (4014), he says at the beginning. Later, he states, "I am stopping my story of Chaunticleer for a moment," *And after wol I telle his aventure* (4376). He digresses, and when he is done says, *Now wol I torne agayn to my sentence* (4404). In a moment he stops again to talk of destiny, and then corrects himself by stating that he will have nothing to do with arguments about free will: *My tale is of a cok, as ye may heere* (4442). Similarly, he brings the mock-heroic passage that follows Chaunticleer's capture to a close with an abrupt, prosaic statement: *Now wole I turne to my tale agayn* (4564), a tale that he insists is not a *folye*. The cumulative effect of all these signals is, by breaking dramatic illusion, to keep us continually aware of the fictional nature of the story. To be sure, the variety of his devices for accomplishing this renders the effect inescapable: not only interruptions of his narrative, but also comparisons between chickens and people, stories within his story, allusions to other stories, and parodies of literary styles. By doing all these things, the Nun's Priest compels us to focus on the mechanics of his art, on his tale as a consciously wrought work of fiction.

It is inviting to speculate that he does this because he is on a pilgrimage whose unifying activity is storytelling. His tale is in one light a comment on that activity, a suggestion that even if the pilgrimage's storytellers do not see it, their fictions are full of moral implications, of hidden truths, and he is thus reminding his listeners to be on the lookout for them. Those truths may not be clearly discernible, or their seriousness may be or may seem to be subverted by comic possibilities, but as in the case of Chaunticleer, the very salvation of the pilgrims may depend upon their ability to interpret what they hear.

STEWART JUSTMAN

# Literal and Symbolic in "The Canterbury Tales"

$I$n a fine article a few years ago, Sheila Delany documented and analyzed "the late medieval attack on analogical thought." The attackers Delany refers to—Jean Buridan, Nicole Oresme, William of Ockham, and others—seek to distinguish between figures of speech and fact. They break with a *symbolic* way of perceiving the world. The analogy "body politic," one argues, has no basis in logic or fact, no real legitimacy; it is a figure of speech, thus a fiction, and one cannot rightly base an argument on it. Chaucer provides the point of departure for Delany's study, although Delany does not actually apply her findings to Chaucer. I propose here to consider the attacks on "analogy" in the *Canterbury Tales* (although I will skirt the belabored issue of figural significance as "determined" by orthodox commentary). The invocation of the Song of Songs in its literal sense in the *Merchant's Tale* (and possibly the *Miller's Tale*); the frequent use of "signes" by Damian and May; Absolon's interpretation of his itching mouth as a "signe" of kissing "atte leeste"; the Wife of Bath's exploitation of the accepted belief that blood in a dream "bitokeneth" gold (D 581); the use in the *Nun's Priest's Tale* of onomatopoeia, words that stand for nothing, but are mere literal sound—all in this sampling can be read as mockery of the symbolic or analogical attitude itself. The tales represent a major break with the view that the world of the senses—the literal world—is necessarily a sacred cipher or "analogy," and that "signs" are necessarily spiritually inscribed. Whereas for St. Bonaventure all literal things are "shadows, echoes, and pictures, the traces, simulacra, and reflection of that First Principle. . . . , signs divinely bestowed which, I say, are exemplars or

From *The Chaucer Review* 14, no. 3. Copyright © 1980 by The Pennsylvania State University Press.

rather exemplifications set before our yet untrained minds," the *Canterbury Tales* abound with mock signs, false exemplifications, allegory that fails.

Commonly, in medieval tradition, an analogy can pass for a literal identity. As one scholar has said, "For both the Middle Ages and the Renaissance, analogy was nothing arbitrary or verbal." The bread of the Eucharist was not just a symbol of Christ's body, an analogy for it; it *was* Christ's body. Again, St. Paul says, "as the body is one and hath many members; and all the members of the body, whereas they are many, yet are one body: so also is Christ." But this is not merely an analogy for merely illustrative purposes. In fact it is not an analogy at all. Paul means it: "Now you are the body of Christ" (1 Cor. 12:27). From "You are like the body of Christ" to "You are the body of Christ." A symbol has become real; an analogy takes on the rights and privileges of an identity. For another medieval ideal of the perfect symbolic body, we may look to Dante. In his ascent through Paradise, Dante sees souls which form the symbols of eagle and rose. In each case the symbol literally is the larger community. The symbol of the eagle stands for law and literally embodies law, in that all the souls that make it up have taken their proper places. To the modern reader, the rose may signify transfigured sexuality. But the great transfiguration that has made the rose is also an actual display of something much like what we understand by "sublimation," the redirection of will according to "law" and in the mode of symbols. In each case the symbol is more than a symbol. It is itself real. It is a claim for the reality of analogical thought.

Griselda's obligation to her word (which transcends her obligation to her children), the irrevocable "sentence" pronounced by Virginius, the power of oaths in the *Friar's* and *Summoner's Tales*, the Pardoner's rhyme of "swere" and "totere" (C 473-74)—all attest to the idea that words are more than merely "verbal," that they are real, formal acts—a contract with reality. On the other hand, though, we have the Reeve's statement, "whan we may nat doon, than wol we speke" (A 3881); Symkyn's challenge to the clerks, "Lat se now if this place may suffise, / Or make it rowm with speche, as is youre gise" (A 4125-26); the absurd verbal dilation of the *Nun's Priest's Tale*, as opposed to the brevity of this "tale" within it: "If thou tomorwe wende, / Thow shalt be dreynt; my tale is at an ende" (B² 4271-72). In these cases words are vain, inauthentic fictions that stand for nothing. The *Canterbury Tales* offers many examples of inauthentic fictions and figures stripped of real authority.

As we might expect, Chaucer's Wife of Bath is particularly adept at parody of analogical thought. Borrowing from St. Jerome's *Adversus Iovinianum* (I,7), she seizes on an analogy showing the superiority of virginity to marriage—an analogy that is indeed merely illustrative. "I nyl envye no virginitee," she says. "Lat hem be breed of pured whete-seed, / And lat us wyves hoten barly breed. . ." (D 142-44). In this hypothetical analogy of Jerome's, neither the wheat bread nor the barley bread has any absolute importance in itself. Any similar pairing of better and lesser terms would do. In other words, Jerome does not really mean "barley bread" literally. But the Wife of Bath takes him at his literal word. Jumping from Jerome to the Evangelist Mark, the Wife goes on, "And yet with barly-breed, Mark telle kan, / Oure Lord Jhesu refresshed many a man": thus "wyves" have God's favor, too. By splicing two authorities and giving Jerome's figure of speech more truth-value than it deserves, she turns a mere illustration demeaning marriage into positive evidence endorsing marriage; she alleges scriptural authority for personal license. (On top of it all, she has got her Evangelists wrong. Mark does not recount the miracle of the loaves, but John.) Even though "analogy was nothing arbitrary or verbal" to the Middle Ages, the Wife, especially with the formula "lat us . . . hoten," calls ironic attention to the purely symbolic, verbal character of Jerome's analogy, minor as the analogy is. By taking a figure of speech with ironic literalism, she parodies analogical thought, and at the same time nullifies moral controls, or what Chaucer calls "auctoritee."

The canny wife of the *Shipman's Tale* works very much the same trick on St. Paul, Jerome's chief authority in *Adversus Iovinianum*. She, too, abuses a figure of speech, and to grasp the trick we must know that "to pay one's debt" is a euphemism for "to have sex with one's spouse." Paul says, "Let the husband render the debt to his wife: and the wife also in like manner to the husband" (1 Cor. 7:3). By way of appeasing her husband's displeasure over her squandering his hundred franks, the wife cajoles him: "Ye han mo slakkere dettours than am I!" (B² 1603). Here she refers to a literal, monetary debt that she will "pay off" in bed. The term that Paul uses figuratively, euphemistically, the wife here uses literally, in the manner of the Wife of Bath's trick with barley bread. If I fail to pay, she says, "score it upon my taille" (1606)—a salacious pun on tally/tail. Both this wife and the Wife of Bath are of the young, well-to-do middle class; both bring monetary calculation to sex; both subvert the authority of tradition. These women bring to mind Marx and Engels's contention that

> The bourgeoisie, wherever it has got the upper hand, has put an end to all feudal, patriarchal, idyllic relations. It has pitilessly torn asunder the motley feudal ties that bound man to his "natural superiors". . . . The bourgeoisie has torn away from the family its sentimental veil, and has reduced the family relation to a mere money relation. . . . All fixed, fast-frozen relations, with their train of ancient and venerable prejudices and opinions, are swept away.

For the Middle Ages, among those "fixed, fast-frozen relations" is the analogical or figurative relation. By reducing the figurative to the literal, the Wife of

Bath and the wife of the *Shipman's Tale* parody the analogical relation, and implicitly attack "ancient and venerable prejudices," or traditional moral controls.

## II

Symbols, "figures," are indeed bound up with moral controls, as medieval commentators on the Song of Songs knew. The Song of Songs is the great locus of medieval exegesis. In its exegetical history, which extended beyond the Middle Ages, it was the subject of hundreds of commentaries. A glance at just one verse may suggest why: "My beloved put his hand through the key hole, and my bowels were moved at his touch" (v.4). This is strong stuff. Commentators evidently felt a need to domesticate it. More, they felt they could make a clear gain out of it. Exegesis here could turn a potential liability into an actual credit by showing that what appears to be the most dangerous part of the Old Testament is really the most mystically fruitful of all, that what appears to be a celebration of profane love is really a celebration of Christ's love for the Church, or the soul. By insisting that the Song of Songs is written in symbols—in code—the Middles Ages brought it under control. Today "code" still implies both a system of controls (the legal code) and a system of symbols (the Morse code). In the case of the Song of Songs, symbol *is* control. Kenneth Burke's claim that the negative ("involving the 'thou-shalt-not's' . . . of law and conscience") is itself a "symbolic invention" brings to mind the exegesis of the Song of Songs, where to prohibit (sexuality, in this case) and to construe symbolically amount to the same thing.

In a more general sense, too, it can be said that symbols are bound up with moral controls. It is a commonplace in the study of metaphor that encompassing metaphorical constructs control us as much as we control them. The chain of being—Theseus' "cheyn of love"—is, after all, a *chain*. Authority finds good uses for controlling metaphors like this. For example, the great analogy of the "body politic," which pre-dates the Middle Ages, puts everything in its "natural" place under the "head," and so is in the interest of the "upper" orders. It is for this reason that organicist metaphors have been a staple of conservative ideology. Gower says that the "membres" "scholden bowe" to the head. What David Edge has said of technological folk metaphors holds true for master metaphors like the organicist metaphor as well: they "conspire to consolidate our tendency so to conceptualize the world that its supposed categories impose upon us . . . order and control. . . ."

Sublimation, in the Freudian sense, also demonstrates the relation between symbols and controls. Sublimation depends on the transfiguration of literal content. It gives impulses *figurative* expression. "The instinctual demands, being forced aside from direct satisfaction, are compelled to take new directions which lead to substitute satisfactions, and in the course of these *détours* they may become desexualized and their connection with their original instinctual aims may weaken." Dante's love for the earthly Beatrice is legitimized as it is transfigured into a "higher" sublimated love. The Song of Songs is legitimzed by its "higher" spiritual content. Reinterpreted, the letter is the same as it always was, but it is seen in a new spirit. Unfortunately, though, shifts in "spirit" can just as well be ironic or parodic. St. Augustine says, "Now irony indicates by inflection what it wishes to be understood, as when we say to a man who is doing evil, 'You are doing well'." If a sixty-year-old lecher were to marry a twenty-year-old wench and entice her, in a strongly "inflected" citation from the Song of Songs, into a pleasure garden to perform things even he will not do in his bedroom—in this case something very much like the idea of moral controls will have been mocked. To undo the exegesis of the Song of Songs would not only offend against the idea of Christian exegesis, but would also imply an unmasking of impulses which medieval Christendom judged were better sublimated. We can call old January a literalist in that he ironically restores the literal sense of the Song of Songs (E 2138 48).

The principle of sublimation—of symbol as control—would seem to apply to a social structure also. One or two examples will confirm the extent to which social controls involve symbolism, and may suggest the antiauthoritarian bias of the attack on symbolism in the *Canterbury Tales*. (We can expect some debunking of the figurative on a pilgrimage whose "figure" of authority is earthy, burly Harry Bailly—who seems to have been a literal, historical person.) My examples are modern, but the principle—the symbolic nature of authority—is basic, and holds good for Chaucer's time as well.

Suppose that two people, working together, commit a crime. One of them, though, turns out to have been an informer. He is not even tried, while his "accomplice" is convicted. Although the two committed literally the same act, the informer did not "really" commit a crime. His act is legitimized as having been symbolic; it was displaced "upward," undertaken in the "higher" interests of authority.

Again, if you hit someone over the head, you have committed a crime, but if the police do, in the line of duty, they have not committed a crime. Although the two acts are physically the same, their meaning is different. We could say that the acts are the same in letter, but different in spirit. As the police badge indicates, the police are a symbol of Law itself. In theory at least, their hitting one over the head is the result of no personal dispute whatsoever. The violent impulse, expressed at a "higher" level, under a new aegis, is now acceptable to the State. More, it is a positive benefit to the

State. For while aggression in a personal, unauthorized capacity is a social danger, aggression contained in a policing capacity strengthens social controls. Chaucer's Melibee learns that vengeance "aperteneth and longeth al oonly to the juges" (B² 2659). Just as medieval Christianity turned the potentially dangerous Song of Songs to its own gainful uses, so the State turns a danger into a gain, and both by the same means: by the operation of symbolism. When Aleyn in the Reeve's Tale cites a "lawe that says thus, / That gif a man in a point be agreved, / That in another he sal be releved" (A 4180-82), he subverts both senses of the word "code." In that he ignores the distinction between "personal" violence and "higher," authorized violence, he shows a poor grasp of the symbolic function; in that his legal maxim establishes no formal correspondence whatever between crime and punishment, it can hardly be part of a system of controls. As is clear in the context of the Reeve's Tale, this "lawe" annuls law.

When the police are violent, their acts are to be understood symbolically: the police stand for Law. The informer's act, too, is to be symbolically understood. It was because of the transcendent priority of Law itself that the Middle Ages regarded rebellion as the first and worst of crimes: it was the ur-Crime, the crime of Lucifer. Rebellion is a crime against Law with a capital "L"—an abstraction, symbolic in nature; all other crimes are crimes against this or that law with a lower-case "l." St. Augustine understood that social order is a matter of symbols: "the useful and necessary institutions established by men with men include . . . innumerable kinds of signs without which human society could not or could not easily function. . . ." It is because social order depends on symbols that for Dante counterfeiting coins is a worse crime than murder. It is more far-reaching. As opposed to Dante, Chaucer is fascinated with counterfeiting—with false relics, bogus alchemy, counterfeit keys, unauthentic statements, literary falsifications, false fronts of all kinds. And a counterfeit is a copy of the "letter" in the wrong "spirit." We will see that puns, irony, and impersonation all involve counterfeiting in this sense, and we will see the connection between symbols and authority confirmed often in Chaucer.

## III

Among the counterfeiters is May of the Merchant's Tale. Using "warm wex" (E 2117), she counterfeits a key to January's pleasure garden in order to set up the pear-tree liaison. Earlier in the tale, January had thought that a young bride would be manipulable "Right as men may warm wex with handes plye" (E 1430). The reduction from "like warm wax" to literal warm wax amounts to something like a literalization of a figure of speech, with an ironic twist, recalling the ploys of the Wife of Bath and the wife of the *Shipman's Tale*. Indeed the current of ironic literalism in the *Merchant's Tale* is strong. It is said that "love is blynd" (E 1598); accordingly, January goes literally blind. Women are ironically extolled as the "fruyt" of a man's "tresor" (E 1270); May claims that pregnant women have an inordinate desire for fruit (E 2335-37), and cuckolds January in a pear tree. A priest tells May to be like Rebecca (E 1704), and she answers the charge only to this narrow, literal extent: like Rebecca, she engineers a plot to deceive a blind, old husband. Again, January, in his burlesque of the Song of Songs, implicitly rejects the idea that the Song of Songs is encoded as a "sign" of a "higher" truth. Immediately after January's serenade, May cynically makes a "signe" (E 2150) to Damian; the two also converse in "privee signes" (E 2105) and in "signes" she makes with her "fynger" (E 2209)—acts insignificant enough except for their nearness to January's rendition of the Song of Songs and for the teller's emphasis on the idea of signs. None of the principals has any sense of a sign as something spiritually inscribed. And the names "January" and "May" suggest that these two are, after all, mock allegorization or "signs" themselves.

There are similar assaults on symbolism scattered through the *Canterbury Tales*. The Miller says he has a tale about a carpenter and his wife, who the reader at once assumes stand for—symbolize—Joseph and Mary. What other carpenter and wife team was there? In fact they stand for no one, or old John is a brutal parody of Joseph of the Cherry-Tree Carol—demythologizing in either case. In this tale, too, Absolon's dream "signe" is fulfilled ironically; in an instance of "anti-typology" (perhaps similar to the Merchant's reverse typology, in which figurative fruit is reduced to literal fruit), a "plowshare" is turned into a "sword"; and the water for which Nicholas calls has no "higher" significance, no sacred associations whatsoever, even though old John has been gulled into believing that it does: it is just lower-case water. Apparently the Miller has little regard for symbolism, as he has little respect for the authority of the Host. The *Friar's Tale* appears to reinforce the essential connection between authority and symbolism in that it features a summoner who abuses both. This roving extortionist works "withouten mandement" (D 1346) or without authorization, and when, in his travels, he overhears an oath like "The devel have al," he construes it quite literally as a material gain for himself (since he and the devil have agreed to divide the spoils), regardless of the spirit in which the oath was uttered. "Authorization" is itself something symbolic, so that it is at least poetically just, if not logically necessary, that one who sneers at "authorization" should be dead to something equally symbolic, "entente." For his part, the Manciple, who gathers all crows into one "higher" ancestral exemplar, one Crow, mocks exemplarism as he jests with the authority of Ovid (his source) and of his mother (the voice of proverbial wisdom). In this superbly ironic tale, Apollo makes a lesson of the crow for speaking the truth as the crow himself witnessed it: Apollo has been cuckolded. The tale not only vindicates the first-hand experience of the crow as against the absurdity of ritually invoked "auctoritee," but also ridicules the idea that there is a symbol in everything down to the very crows, that Nature is a book of lessons, that (as Bonaventure says) "All creatures of this sensible world" are "signs" and "exemplifications."

Chaucer's Pardoner is himself a false exemplification, a counterfeit. Although he makes himself out to be the authorized representative of the Church, there is no evidence that he is accountable to anyone. One irony of the "signes" (C 419) by which he indicates to a congregation which parishioner he is defaming is that he is really a false "sign" himself, as are his relics. Ironically, the Pardoner's own tale confirms the connection of symbols and controls. It concerns three young "rioters" who reject both. They undertake to kill Death himself. It is clear that they do not understand the difference between an abstraction and a real person, any more than the Mad Hatter does when he cautions Alice against beating Time when she practices her music. In this sense they are literalists. An old man directs them to Death under a nearby tree, where they find bushels of gold over which they then kill one another. They pay the price for their failure to decode the old man's instructions. They did not understand how gold could "represent" death, and it stands to reason that "rioters" who have little sense of symbolism do not acknowledge loyalty to any abstraction like a social unit, even one of their own making. In this sense the Pardoner's is "a moral tale" (C 460), a fact underscored by all of the teller's sermonizing. But the issue does not rest there. In the Pardoner's windy digression from his tale proper almost as soon as it begins, we sense the power of words to run away from reality—as opposed, say, to the words "Diligite Iustitiam Qui Iudicatis Terram" which Dante sees actually formed by souls in his ascent through Paradise, words which are real acts themselves. The approximately equal proportion in the *Pardoner's Tale* of windy sermonizing—words unnecessary to and apart from "plot"—to the "plot" itself may recall a modern idea, the first fact of language: that words are, after all, a "digression" from reality in that they "are *not* the things they stand for." Words are of a symbolic order a quantum apart from lived experience. There is nothing objectionable in an immoral man's telling a moral tale, but that act clearly implies that words are disconnected from reality. Unlike analogical thought, but like the Wife of Bath and the wife of the *Shipman's Tale*, the Pardoner may ironically remind us of the purely symbolic, un-real character of words. As a professional talker, the Pardoner finds it easy enough to exploit the falsity inherent in language.

In the *Nun's Priest's Tale* words do run away from reality. The overbalance of "unnecessary" words to "plot" is extreme: the "plot" is meager, all but lost, while there is an enormous overlay of "unnecessary" words. And if, as Kenneth Burke says, "There is an implied sense of negativity in the ability to use words at all" (in that words are *not* what they stand for), in the *Nun's Priest's Tale* we are told that there was *not* as much lamentation in Troy as there was at Chauntecleer's kidnapping, that "Jakke Straw and his meynee" ($B^2$ 4584) did *not* make such a clamor as there was in the barnyard. All of these words finally do *not* "equal" the reality the tale describes. And animals can*not* talk. Ironically, to mock words—that is, symbols—the Nun's Priest uses words in abundance. It is with sounds that symbolize *nothing*, mere onomatopoeia, that we come closest in this tale to the reality under the overlay of words:

> He *chukketh* whan he hath a corn yfounde. . . .
>
> He was war of this fox, that lay ful lowe.
> Nothyng ne liste hym thanne for to crowe,
> But cride anon, *"Cok! cok!"* and up he sterte. . . .
> $$(B^2\ 4372,\ 4465\text{-}67)$$

At these "moments of truth," language is not symbolic. The Nun's Priest, in this respect like the Miller, has little use for symbolism. Despite the fantastic possibilities of the medieval dream vision, Chauntecleer's dream is simply a preview of the fox that would carry him off from the barnyard—a preview *literally* accurate down to the black tips. If the dream fox only stands for a fox, the teller of this tale does not say conclusively what his tale stands for, if anything, and this indeterminacy itself is an affront to the idea that *visibilia* bear the legible signature of, bear an analogical relation to, *invisibilia*. In the end the Nun's Priest disingenuously reneges on his authority as teller (thus suggesting a connection between the matter of symbolism and authority), and throws the responsibility for making sense of his tale on his audience. Take the fruit (that is, the wheat) and leave the chaff, he says: in effect an open invitation to make of his tale what one will. I believe that the *Nun's Priest's Tale* really concerns the authenticity of the commonplace, the chaff, and of the literalist perception. It shows that high Latin culture has no place in the barnyard, and that the barnyard is no place to look for moral signification. All creation is not a hieroglyph, or, if there is a book of nature, we cannot read it.

The argument that Chaucer was not necessarily endorsing the putative "wheat" within the "chaff" gains strength from the fact that he himself, in his literary borrowings, did not always take the "wheat." Chaucer saw a spiritualized version of Ovid, the *Ovide moralisé*; but when he mined material from this work, he took stories and left behind the moralizations which told what the stories stand for. He took the chaff and left the wheat. One scholar says of the allegorical sections of the *Ovide moralisé* that Chaucer "seems to have ignored them." There could be an exclamation point after that comment, because in ignoring the moralizations, Chaucer not only put his material to an unauthorized use, but also ignored the idea of the "higher" symbolic dimension which is essential to strategies of moral control. Still, Chaucer was not a subversive. Everyone knows he had the trust of the king. He wrote nothing of substance about the great Peasant Revolt of 1381, even though he may have watched a mob storm into London under his window. But Chaucer was not doctrinaire, either. There is not the slightest justification for assuming that he was bound, *ipso facto*, by any prior exegetical tradition. He knew the absurdity of conventional moralizing (even though that was to continue into the Renaissance). He knew that the letter does not necessarily kill, since he has an unprincipled scoundrel in the *Summoner's Tale* say that it does (D 1794). And he knew that the literal might not rest easily with the symbolic—a point which his own wretched *Tale of Melibee* confirms.

In this "tale" Melibee comes home one day to find that three of his old enemies have broken into his house, wounded his daughter, and left her for dead. We are told later that the three stand for the world, the flesh, and the devil. This much is, perhaps, simple enough, even if the allegory is starchy. But for most of the "tale," Melibee's exemplary wife urges him to recant his oath of vengeance, give over his enmity toward the wrongdoers, in fact let them off scot free; and Melibee accedes in the end. The problem is that no medieval Christian should be lenient to the world, the flesh, and the devil. Forgiveness is fine as long as the malefactors are literal, mortal beings; but if they are symbolic beings, the "tale" hardly makes sense. As with most of the interesting questions about Chaucer, it is hard to say what he was getting at here. The *Tale of Melibee* is not of his own composition. Chaucer took the letter, but who can prove in what spirit? Perhaps, though, it was not the spirit of his "auctor." Perhaps the *Melibee* is a perfect counterfeit, as, in Augustine's example, the ironic statement "You are doing well" is a perfectly false replica of the straight statement "You are doing well." Everyone today grants that things Chaucer says in his own person are unstraightforward, and he, or someone by his name and with his presumed chubbiness, tells this "tale." Indeed the authority to which Chaucer the creator defers in telling the "tale"—the created Host's—is spurious; thus the act of deference is spurious. The "tale" does suggest, though, that there may be no simple conversion between the literal and the symbolic, that mixing the two can be like interpolating the syntax of one language into another. The *Melibee* also suggests that there may be no easy transcending of the literal. And indeed we are stuck with the literal for better or worse. There can be no literature without it. Nothing can be symbolic unless it is literal first. There can be no "body politic" without literal bodies.

## IV

Any tale, as a verbal structure, is by nature symbolic, and in this sense transcends experience. On the Canterbury pilgrimage, though, many tales do not transcend experience by much. The Reeve takes the *Miller's Tale* to heart as a personal slight and tells a tale in which he has a miller cuckolded. This "fictional" miller excels at "piping" and wrestling, like Robin the Canterbury Miller. Since there are only so many pipe-playing miller-wrestlers, it is fair to assume that the Reeve has Robin the "real" Miller in mind. The Friar and the Summoner, too, carry on personal vendettas of this sort. In each case, the way to "quite" a real person is to put that person into a fiction, to attack an effigy. In that this practice is a displacement of energy into a symbolic mode, it can be called sublimation, but it is surely crude sublimation. Not only is the original impulse of malice perfectly unmodified, but action is *not* displaced to a purely figurative level. The *Friar's Tale* gets physical results: the Summoner "quook for ire" like an aspen leaf after hearing it (D 1667). In fact, the "actual" Summoner disrupts the tale about a fictional summoner, and the Friar returns the favor. Sublimation of hostility works very imperfectly ("I pray to God his nekke mote to-breke," the Reeve says of the Miller); and the proper function of art as conceived in the Middle Ages was not to arouse passions like these, but to still or transfigure them. Again, the Wife of Bath gets back at her fifth husband's *ideas* by ripping leaves from a *physical* book. Given the contradictions of the Wife, it need not surprise us that this is the same woman who ironically summons attention to the purely symbolic character of Jerome's "barley bread" analogy. All of these confusions of the symbolic and the literal—and finally Chaucer's inclusion of himself among *fictional* characters on the pilgrimage—seem to parody the medieval idea of realism, the ascription of reality to ideas. These confusions also imply an affront to three great ideas—that of sublimation, that of exegesis, that of the State—because each of these is a function of the idea of a "higher" symbolic dimension which vitally transcends literal sense experience.

Analogical thought is "realist" in that it assumes the reality of symbols, especially symbols of order, like Dante's eagle. One gloss from a twelfth-century manuscript says that "pedanei" (petty judges) are like "pedes imperatoris" (the feet of the emperor)—a "natural" pun validated by the natural analogy of the "body politic." Profane puns are another case, however. In that punning reduces words to literal sounds, it too can attack the symbolic attitude. Punning in this sense is a verbal equivalent of counterfeiting: the use of a formally identical double in an unorthodox sense. To contend that "gula" (gluttony) is "an indispensable part" of "regula" (the monastic rule) is twice to make light of symbols: first, in reducing a word to mere sounds, as any pun does; but then in making the idea of "regula"—of code, a system of controls and a system of symbols—a joke. Like this Goliardic pun, the word "ars-metrike" in the *Summoner's Tale* (D 2222) calls to mind two words that sound identical: "ars" and "ars." One means "art," as in the liberal "arts"; one means "arse." Although the two words are identical in letter, they are different in meaning. One is Latin; one is Teutonic. One "ars," we might say, is a matter of high culture, the other a matter of "unsublimated" nature. And nature (or instinctual drives) and culture (or moral controls) do not "rhyme," as Freud shows in *Civilization and its Discontents*. Thus the irony of Chaucer's rhymes like "lawe"/"mawe," "proverbes"/"herbes," "nekke"/ "Rebekke" (B 1189-90; D 773-74; E 1703-04). Thus too the irony of his giving birds both bird-speech and human speech in the *Parliament of Fowls*. And thus the irony of the pun on "ars"/"ars" in the *Summoner's Tale*, where a fart (derived from "ars") is to be divided in twelve (by "ars-metrike," arithmetic). Since "all terms for mental states, sociopolitical relationships, and the like are necessarily 'fictions,' in the sense that we must express such concepts by the use of terms borrowed from the realm of the physical," such "returns" of the mental to the physical may amount to an attack on symbolicity itself. Literalistic word-play reduces unlike meanings to like sounds, in defiance of the principle of sublimation, exegesis, and the State—the principle that there is a "higher" symbolic dimension qualitatively unlike literal sense experience.

In the context of medieval spirituality, to pun on verbal twins like "ars"/"ars" is to exploit literal identity in defiance of spiritual difference. It is to reduce words to sounds, to treat words like things. In the *Summoner's Tale* the word "eructavit" (D 1934) is reduced from the Vulgate sense of "uttered forth" to the profane, literal sense of "belched." The wife in the *Shipman's Tale* may be using identity of sound for her own purposes of distortion when she tells her husband that daun John gave her one hundred franks "For cosynage" (B² 1599). To the husband, the word "cosynage" refers to his and the monk's practice of calling one another "cousin." But the wife may intend the meaning of "deception," as in "to cozen" in Shakespeare. All such puns exploit just what medieval commentators feared: the power of sounds, appeals to the senses, "fictions," the literal dimension to deceive. As opposed to the analogical pun of "pedanei"/"pedes," which reveals what is supposed to be a fundamental truth, literalistic word-play exploits the arbitrary and misleading nature of sound. It shows that words are not sacred ciphers.

## V

I will close by considering one inconspicuous slight to symbols which I believe carries the full burden of the attack on symbols in the *Canterbury Tales*.

In Ovid's *Metamorphoses*, when Apollo kills Coronis, we find this description:

> He dropped his lyre, and, as his anger mounted,
> He took the bow, he bent it, fired the arrow
> Into the breast he had felt against his own.
> And the girl groaned, and tugging at the arrow
> Saw her white body redden with crimson stain. . . .

But in the Manciple's tale of the crow, which derives from Ovid, we find:

> His bowe he bente, and sette therinne a flo,
> And in his ire his wyf thanne hath he slayn.
> This is th'effect, ther is namoore to sayn. . . .
> (H 264-66)

The dramatic moment is all but wordless—even though "The wise Plato seith, as ye may rede, / The word moot nede accorde with the dede" (H 207-08)! Although the Manciple had cited "olde bookes" (H 106), he here deflates his old book by passing over its sensationalism. There may be an ironic purpose to the Manciple's roguishness, however. With his "ther is namoore to sayn," the Manciple may imply that, in the end, words, even Ovid's words, will not do. Despite Dante's "Diligite Iustitiam," which is a perfect "adequation" of symbols and fact, symbols are necessarily incommensurate with the reality they represent. Indeed the Manciple's is another of Chaucer's highly digressive, windy tales in which the rhetoric ironically goes one way and the reality another. And in the course of his digressions, the Manciple has reduced the idea of words—of symbolic abstraction—to absurdity. A dishonest woman "of heigh degree," he says, "shal be cleped . . . lady"; while "a povre wenche" shall be "cleped" just that, a wench—even though "Men leyn that oon as lowe as lith that oother" (H 213-22, my emphasis). The implication is that words are meaningless. The Manciple calls attention ironically to the purely symbolic, un-real nature of symbolic abstraction. (He also looks coldly at social station: true to the connection of symbols and social order, when he scants the one he scants the other.) His tale is in fact an ironic attack on speech; to say "ther is namoore to sayn" is in keeping with the moral of the tale, which is "Kepe wel thy tonge" (H 362). If punning reduces words to sounds, the Manciple reduces reality to silence. His tale perfects the attack on symbols in the *Canterbury Tales*. It is a verbal attack on words.

# Chronology

| | |
|---|---|
| ca. 1340–45 | Geoffrey Chaucer born to Agnes and John Chaucer, wealthy property owners. John is a prosperous London wine merchant. |
| 1347 | Chaucer serves as a page to Elizabeth de Burgh, Countess of Ulster. |
| 1359–60 | Chaucer serves in King Edward III's army in France. He is captured, but Edward pays his ransom. |
| ca. 1366 | Chaucer marries Philippa Roet. He begins his association with John of Gaunt, probably through his wife, whose sister, Katherine Swynford, is John of Gaunt's mistress. John Chaucer dies. |
| 1367 | As a member of King Edward III's household, Chaucer receives a royal annuity. |
| ca. 1368–71 | Writes *The Book of the Duchess*. |
| ca. 1372–80 | Writes *Saint Cecilia*, which later becomes the Second Nun's Tale, and some of the Monk's tragedies. |
| 1372–73 | Sent to Genoa and Florence in the service of the King, Chaucer probably becomes acquainted with the writings of Boccaccio, Petrarch, and Dante. He may also have met Petrarch. |
| 1374 | Chaucer moves to the house over the gate of Aldgate. Edward III appoints him Controller of the Customs and Subsidies on Wool for the port of London. |
| 1377 | Chaucer travels to France on the King's behalf. While he is there, Edward III dies and Richard II becomes King. Richard renews Chaucer's customs appointment. |
| ca. 1378–80 | Writes *The House of Fame*. |
| 1378 | Richard II sends Chaucer to Milan, where he renews his acquaintance with Italian literature. |
| ca. 1380–82 | Writes *The Parliament of Fowls*. |
| 1380 | Cecilia Chaumpaigne sues Chaucer for *raptus*. He is cleared of all responsibility. |
| ca. 1382–87 | Chaucer translates Boethius' *Consolation of Philosophy* and writes *Troilus and Criseyde*, *Palamoun and Arcite* (the Knight's Tale), *The Legend of Good Women*, and other shorter works. |

| | |
|---|---|
| 1382–85 | Chaucer is appointed Controller of the Petty Customs, but then begins to phase himself out of his customs jobs by appointing full-time deputies. |
| 1385 | Appointed Justice of the Peace for Kent. |
| 1386 | Chaucer is elected to Parliament as one of the two "Knights of the Shire" to represent Kent. He gives up his house at Aldgate and his controllerships. |
| ca. 1387–92 | Writes the General Prologue and the earlier of the *Canterbury Tales*. |
| 1387 | Philippa Chaucer dies. Chaucer loses his royal annuity and goes into debt. He travels to Calais. |
| 1389 | Richard II appoints Chaucer Clerk of the King's Works. |
| ca. 1390–91 | Chaucer oversees construction and repair on several buildings, including the Tower of London, Westminster Palace, and St. George's Chapel at Windsor Castle. Usually carrying substantial amounts of money, he is robbed several times and possibly is injured. |
| ca. 1391–93 | Writes *A Treatise on the Astrolabe*. |
| 1391 | Chaucer relinquishes his clerkship and is appointed deputy forester of the Royal Forest at North Petherton in Somerset. |
| ca. 1392–95 | Writes most of the *Canterbury Tales* during this period. |
| 1394 | Richard II grants Chaucer a new royal annuity. |
| ca. 1396–1400 | Chaucer writes the latest of the *Tales*, including probably the Nun's Priest's Tale and the Canon's Yeoman's Tale, and several other shorter poems. |
| 1399 | John of Gaunt dies. Henry IV confirms Chaucer's pension and grants him an additional annuity. Chaucer leases a house in the garden of Westminster Abbey. |
| 1400 | Chaucer dies and is buried in Westminster Abbey. |

# Contributors

HAROLD BLOOM, Sterling Professor of the Humanities at Yale University, is the author of *The Anxiety of Influence, Poetry and Repression* and many other volumes of literary criticism. His forthcoming study, *Freud: Transference and Authority*, attempts a full-scale reading of all of Freud's major writings. A MacArthur Prize Fellow, he is the general editor of five series of literary criticism published by Chelsea House. During 1987–88, he was appointed Charles Eliot Norton Professor of Poetry at Harvard University.

GILBERT KEITH CHESTERTON was a prolific English novelist, essayist, poet, and, after his conversion in 1922, Roman Catholic polemicist. He is best remembered for his Father Brown detective stories, for his fantasy novel, *The Man Who Was Thursday* (1908), and for his critical studies of Chaucer, Dickens and Browning.

E. TALBOT DONALDSON was Professor Emeritus of English at Indiana University at Bloomington. He taught at Yale, Columbia, and London University. His editing of Chaucer's poetry (2nd edition, 1975), as well as his commentary, are accessible to scholars and students alike and now serve as the standards for modern Chaucer scholarship and criticism.

DAVID PARKER is Professor of English at the University of Malaya.

ALICE S. MISKIMIN was Professor of English at Yale University. She is now an attorney in New Haven, Connecticut.

DONALD R. HOWARD was Professor of English at Stanford University. He is the author of *Writers and Pilgrims: Medieval Pilgrimage Narratives and their Posterity* (1979).

CHARLES A. OWEN, JR. is Professor of English at the University of Connecticut at Storrs.

SAUL NATHANIEL BRODY is Professor of English at the City University of New York.

STEWART JUSTMAN is Professor of English at the University of Montana.

# Bibliography

Baugh, Albert C., ed. *Chaucer's Major Poetry*. New York: Appleton-Century-Crofts, 1963.

Brewer, Derek S. *Chaucer*. London: Longman, 1973.

_____. *Chaucer and His World*. London: Eyre Methuen, 1978.

_____. *Chaucer and Chaucerians*. University, Ala.: University of Alabama Press, 1966.

_____, ed. *Writers and Their Background: Geoffrey Chaucer*. Athens, Ohio: Ohio University Press, 1975.

Byran, W. F., and Dempster, Germaine, eds. *Sources and Analogues of Chaucer's Canterbury Tales*. Chicago: University of Chicago Press, 1941.

Cawley, A. C. *Chaucer's Mind and Art*. Edinburgh: Oliver and Boyd, 1969.

Chesterton, G. K. *Chaucer*. New York: Greenwood Press, 1969.

Coghill, Nevill. *The Poet Chaucer*. London: Oxford University Press, 1949.

Crow, Martin M., and Olson, Clair C., eds. *Chaucer Life-Records*. Oxford: Clarendon Press, 1966.

Donaldson, E. Talbot. *Speaking of Chaucer*. New York: Norton, 1970.

_____, ed. *Chaucer's Poetry*. 2nd ed. New York: John Wiley and Sons, 1975.

Faulkner, Dewey R., ed. *Twentieth Century Interpretations of the Pardoner's Tale*. Englewood Cliffs, New Jersey: Prentice-Hall, Inc., 1973.

French, Robert Dudley. *A Chaucer Handbook*. New York: Appleton-Century-Crofts, 1947.

Fyler, John M. *Chaucer and Ovid*. New Haven and London: Yale University Press, 1979.

Gardner, John. *The Life and Times of Chaucer*. New York: Knopf, 1977.

_____. *The Poetry of Chaucer*. Carbondale, Ill.: Southern Illinois University Press, 1977.

Howard, Donald R. *The Idea of The Canterbury Tales*. Berkeley: University of California Press, 1976.

Kelly, Henry Ansgar. *Love and Marriage in the Age of Chaucer*. Ithaca: Cornell University Press, 1975.

Kolve, V. A. *Chaucer and the Imagery of Narrative*. Palo Alto: Stanford University Press, 1984.

Lawler, Traugott. *The One and The Many in the Canterbury Tales*. Hamden, Connecticut: Archon Books, 1980.

Manly, J. M. *Some New Light on Chaucer*. New York: Henry Holt and Co., 1926.

_____, ed. *Chaucer's Canterbury Tales*. New York: Henry Holt and Co., 1928.

Manly, J. M., and Rickert, Edith, eds. *The Text of the Canterbury Tales*. 8 vols. Chicago: University of Chicago Press, 1940.

McCall, John P. *Chaucer Among the Gods: The Poetics of Classical Myth*. University Park: Pennsylvania State University Press, 1979.

Miskimin, Alice. *The Renaissance Chaucer*. New Haven and London: Yale University Press, 1975.

Morrison, Theodore, ed. *The Portable Chaucer*. New York: Viking, 1949.

Muscatine, Charles. *Chaucer and The French Tradition*. Berkeley and London: The University of California Press, 1969.

Owen, Charles A., Jr. *Pilgrimage and Storytelling in the Canterbury Tales*. Norman, Oklahoma: The University of Oklahoma Press, 1977.

Payne, F. Anne. *Chaucer and Menippean Satire*. Madison: University of Wisconsin Press, 1981.

Payne, Robert O. *The Key of Remembrance: A Study of Chaucer's Poetics*. Westport, Connecticut: Greenwood Press, 1973.

Robertson, D. W., Jr. *A Preface to Chaucer*. Princeton: Princeton University Press, 1962.

Robinson, F. N., ed. *The Works of Geoffrey Chaucer*. 2nd ed. Boston: Houghton Mifflin Co., 1957.

Root, Robert Kilburn. *The Book of Troilus and Criseide*. Princeton: Princeton University Press, 1926.

Rose, Donald M. *New Perspectives in Chaucer Criticism*. Norman, Oklahoma: Pilgrim Books, Inc., 1981.

Ross, Thomas W. *Chaucer's Bawdy*. New York: E. P. Dutton and Co., 1972.

Rowland, Beryl. *A Companion to Chaucer Studies*. New York: Oxford University Press, 1979.

Schoeck, Richard V., and Taylor, Jerome, eds. *Chaucer Criticism*. 2 vols. Notre Dame, Indiana: University of Notre Dame Press, 1961.

Scott, A. F. *Who's Who in Chaucer*. New York: Taplinger Publishing Company, 1974.

Skeat, W. W., ed. *The Works of Geoffrey Chaucer*. Oxford: The Clarendon Press, 1926.

Spurgeon, Caroline F. E. *500 Years of Chaucer Criticism and Allusion, 1357–1900*. New York: Russell and Russell, 1960.

Tatlock, J. S. P. *The Mind and Art of Chaucer*. Norman, Oklahoma: The University of Oklahoma Press, 1968.

Wagenknecht, Edward. *The Personality of Chaucer*. Norman, Oklahoma: The University of Oklahoma Press, 1968.

————, ed. *Chaucer, Modern Essays in Criticism*. Oxford: Oxford University Press, 1959.

# Acknowledgments

"The Greatness of Chaucer" by G. K. Chesterton from *Chaucer* by G. K. Chesterton, copyright © 1932 by Faber & Faber Ltd., © 1969 by A. P. Watt Ltd. Reprinted by permission.

"The Ending of 'Troilus'" by E. Talbot Donaldson from *Speaking of Chaucer* by E. Talbot Donaldson, copyright © 1970, 1977 by E. Talbot Donaldson. Reprinted by permission of The Athlone Press.

"The Effect of the 'Merchant's Tale'" by E. Talbot Donaldson from *Speaking of Chaucer* by E. Talbot Donaldson, copyright © 1970, 1977 by E. Talbot Donaldson. Reprinted by permission of the Athlone Press.

"Can We Trust the Wife of Bath?" by David Parker from *The Chaucer Review* 4, no. 2, copyright © 1969 by The Pennsylvania State University Press. Reprinted by permission.

"From Medieval to Renaissance: Some Problems in Historical Criticism" by Alice S. Miskimin from *The Renaissance Chaucer* by Alice S. Miskimin, copyright © 1975 by Yale University. Reprinted by permission of Yale University Press.

"The Idea of *The Canterbury Tales*" by Donald R. Howard from *The Idea of The Canterbury Tales* by Donald R. Howard, copyright © 1976 by the Regents of the University of California. Reprinted by permission of the University of California Press.

"The Importance of the Literal" by Charles A. Owen, Jr., from *Pilgrimage and Storytelling in The Canterbury Tales* by Charles A. Owen, Jr., copyright © 1977 by University of Oklahoma Press. Reprinted by permission.

"Truth and Fiction in the 'Nun's Priest's Tale'" by Saul Nathaniel Brody from *The Chaucer Review* 14, no. 1, copyright © 1979 by The Pennsylvania State University Press. Reprinted by permission.

"Literal and Symbolic in *The Canterbury Tales*" by Stewart Justman from *The Chaucer Review* 14, no. 3, copyright © 1980 by The Pennsylvania State University Press. Reprinted by permission.

# Index